DELIVERANCE MANUAL

DELIVERANCE MANUAL

A JOURNEY OUT OF SANTERIA INTO ROYALTY

By Pastor Dennis Perez

Mill City Press

MCP Books
2301 Lucien Way #415
Maitland, FL 32751
407.339.4217
www.millcitypress.net

Printed in the United States of America

ISBN-13: 978-1-6312-9600-0
Ebook: 978-1-6312-9601-7

DEDICATION

I want to dedicate this book to the one that I've been searching for most of my life. I looked for you in friends, I looked for you in music, I looked for you in women, I looked for you in drugs & alcohol, I looked for you in Religion and I looked for you in family. I knew from the first time that I met you, that you were the one. You filled the emptiness that I had deep within, your perfect love I never be away from you my Yeshua Ha-Mashiac (Jesus Christ of Nazareth) As I write this dedication I shed tears of joy and gratitude just fills my heart. Thank You ABBA Father & The Holy Spirit (Ruach Ha Ko-Desh)

To my beautiful wife Esther, I Thank You for your unwavering Love, Commitment and Integrity.

Special Thanks

I'm truly grateful & Honor the following people who have contributed to my development as a servant of God. In no particular order:

- Andrew Butler for guiding me in the early days of my walk
- Maria Figueroa for fasting & interceding for me when I was still in the world
- To the Martinez Family of Cristo En Las Antillas for being my first Pastorial Teachers.
- Apostle Elbi & Lourdes Castillo, Congregation El Olam, I thank and Honor Apostle Elbi for teaching me the Torah, for my Deliverance from Santeria, Teaching me the Word from a Hebrew Perspective, Anointing me as a Pastor. Words cannot describe the gratitude I have for you.
- Pastor Veronica Duran & Prophetess Ruth Jimenez teaching me intercession & deliverance strategies

- Apostle Polo Velez for your consistant Godly counsel
- Apostle Ken Griffith for being an example of Professionalism in ministry
- Apostle Ryan LeStrange I thank you for your kindness, your words of encouragement, your Anointed Teachings and Impartations, I Thank You !!!
- My Apostle Benjamin Smith, Embassy International thank you for being used to shift us to our Kingdom Mandate
- Abel Castillo for his Anointed Worship, Yadira Castillo for your supernatural dance ministry, Obed Castillo's humbleness & eclectic percussion Anointing, Evelin Gomez being an example to Honoring your parents.
- Special Thanks to the Julia, Jimenez, Pillott, Claussell, Sanchez families

TABLE OF CONTENTS

PREFACE

I received a prophetic word for the Lord Jesus Christ in November 2017 that I was going to write a Deliverance Manual. At the time I really did'nt understand how I was going to write a book. Even though I had personally been through a few sessions myself. I was a part of many deliverance sessions since I came to the Lord in 2011. The Lord kept reminding me about the book that he told me to write. Then it hit me using the model of the Mel Gibson directed blockbuster movie. The **Passion of The Christ** dramatically **captures** the last 12 hours of Christ's life on Earth.

The 6 months before I was saved was a good starting point. I wanted to walk the people reading this book what I went through. Searching for answers to what I was feeling in midst of being neckdeep into the Santeria Occult Religion / Catholicism. Because like most of you think that you know who God is, who Jesus Christ is, it's all based on what your parents, family, friends or church you were exposed to. I find it pretty amazing that God used Joel Olsteen the well know TV Preacher, whom many call a Prosperity Preacher to have me confess Jesus Christ as my Lord & Savior. This gave God the legal right over my soul which ignited the battle of deception & truth in the battle field of my mind. As the war raged all around me I was being taught to listen to that little small voice deep within me.

The 1 ½ year time frame the testimonial portion captured also contains the 10 years serving the Lord, studing the Torah / Bible from a Hebrew Perspective Experiences, Revelations in Prayer & Fasting. I didn't include the supernatural experiences I went through in this same 1 ½ year time frame. I believe there's an additional book that will discuss those experiences, secrets revealed, along with other relevant Deliverance Teachings that the Body of Christ needs. This mindset of the word Deliverance is so much more that what people think. My father in-law / spiritual father Apostle Elbi Castillo (RIP) was doing this over 38 years in NYC. He never sounded the Shofar claiming to be the only one to be doing deliverance. The motto of Apostle Elbi was do what ever Yeshua (Jesus Christ) did when he walked the earth.

In closing I hear so many theologians and people in ministry like to use the term "In the Original Greek". When referring to the books of the New Testament were all written in Greek as far as scholars can tell. There is no evidence that any New Testament books were written in Hebrew. Even many of the Old Testament quotations in the New are taken from the Greek Septuagint version of the Old Testament rather than the original Hebrew.

I was taught that the New Testament was written in Hebrew. So I decided to go before the Sprit of Truth" the Holy Spirit and ask Him to confirm if the New Testament was written in Greek or Hebrew)

John 16:13 (NIV)

> [13] But when he, **the Spirit of truth, comes, he will guide you into all the truth**. He will not speak on his own; he will speak only what he hears, and he will tell you what is yet to come.

The response that I received was that it was written in Hebrew.

Father God in the name of Jesus Christ of Nazareth, I Declare, Proclaim & Decree a Divine Order of Protection and cover them with the Blood of Jesus Christ upon every person & their entire family named in this book, every person who reads this book, every person, company, store who sells this book and their families in the Name of Jesus Christ of Nazareth. In the name of Jesus Christ of Nazareth I cancel every satanic decree, order, curse every person associated with this book. I Bind & Rebuke the Spirit of Revenge, Vengence, Retailation, Angel / Spirit of Death and prohibit each of you to come near every person associated with this book. I seal this Decree with Esther 8:8 in Jesus Christ Name.

Chapter 1

THE BEGINNING

The Lord spoke to me on several occasions to write a book / manual so to speak on deliverance. I said to myself there are so many books on the subject of deliverance. I started to recall the books that I have already read on the subject matter. Then after a couple of months of gathering thoughts and writing down experiences, it finally hit me. I thought about the months before I came to the Lord and all the way until a year and a half after. I honestly can say this was the most difficult time in my entire life. But if I had to target a specific time I must say it was the six months before I was saved. I went through some terrifying moments that now I know were intense spiritual warfare for my very soul.

During this period there wasn't any YouTube video tutorials, manuals, books, e-books, or even testimonies, there were'nt definitely no step-by-step instructions on how to get delivered from Santeria and Catholicism. I didn't know anything about deliverance, I didn't know that the Bible contained all the keys that I needed to set me free. Upon hearing the word "deliverance" the first thing that most people would imagine is the scene straight out of the movie The Exorcist with the priest throwing holy water on the little girl.

There were no resources for a person living in the world away from the things of God that you can turn to for help. Even all the people that I knew didn't have a clue as to how to be delivered. My sister who was serving God for about ten years as a Christian didn't know. The only truth that she did say was that there's no power greater than Jesus Christ. But with 20/20 hindsight I can honestly say that the Lord prepared me for a time such as this. I believe that we're about to see secrets of the kingdom of darkness being brought to the light to set God's people free.

Let's talk about my initiation into Santeria

My story in Espiritismo / Santeria began in 1995, and to God Father and my Lord and Savior Jesus Christ of Nazareth be the glory and all the praise, it ended in 2011. The first time that I went to a medium was in a town called Rio Grande, Puerto Rico. The place was set up in a garage like structure in the back. I walked in this room with about with about 5 people. The Lady was called La Madrina (Godmother) This lady preferred method of divination is called Espiritismo (she utilized a bowl full of water and a crystal ball to tell me about my life. In Santeria it's normally a Babalawo (padrino, or godfather). She started to pray her facial expression looked as if she was possessed and began to tell me truths mixed with half truths, which was nothing more than divination by a python type of demon or spirit.

I honestly believe every person who visits psychic, mediums, tarot card / crystal ball readers, Santeros / Babalawos, Paleros and the list goes on. They wonder how is that they know all these things about me? I remember on my very first visit saying to myself this must be of God. The devil is a liar! Satan and his demons have been around since the beginning, they know everything about you and your family. Because God, Jesus, The Holy Spirit, the angels, the Devil, fallen angels & demons they never sleep.

Let's look at the bible for clarification on who is speaking when a person states they're telling you your future, or giving you a reading. The bible states in Revelation 19:10 the following:

Revelation 19:10 (KJV)

[10] And I fell at his feet to worship him. And he said unto me, See thou do it not: I am thy fellowservant, and of thy brethren that have the testimony of Jesus: worship God: for the testimony of Jesus is the spirit of prophecy.

What you just read the Apostle John's spirit was brought up to Heaven. When he saw an angel the bible states that he fell at his feet to worship him. The angel immediately told not to that "I Am a fellow servants" Listen closely and understand it is the People that have and do the following:

- Have the testimony of Jesus Christ.
- Worship God (in Spirit & in Truth John 4:24)
- The testimony of Jesus is the spirit of prophecy.

So only the People who have accepted Jesus Christ as their Lord & Savior and possess the (3) qualities in **Revelations 19:10** are the only ones that carry the spirit of prophecy.

Even in the church there's people that do not carry the Testimony of Jesus Christ and want to come to you to give you a so call word from the Lord. We are living in a time when everyone claims to be a prophet. People that want to do and live what ever way that they feel like living. They want to come to church whenever they feel like it, They don't submit to their Pastors, Leaders, Husbands, Wives and Authorities established by God. They have this other life that inconsistent with what the bible states how we have to live if we want to go to heaven after this life.

Any person that does not carry the testimony of Jesus Christ the words that are coming out of their mouths are nothing more than DIVINATION.

When a person who has accepted Jesus Christ as their savior and begin to live a life that does not represent the testimony of Jesus Christ. If they're not careful a spirit of divination can come upon them and confuse them to think it's God speaking to them. They may get dreams, visions or even think that is God Speaking

I moved to New Jersey (NJ) in the fall of 1995 to begin my career as a Correctional Officer. I drove from NJ to NYC in the spring of 1996 to meet and get a reading from this Cuban Babalawo. Before I get into what happened next for the sake of people that don't know what Santeria is let me explain. **Santería**, also known as **Regla de Ocha**, **Regla de Ifá**, or **Lucumí**, is an Afro-American religion that developed in Cuba between the 16th and 19th centuries. It arose through a process of syncretism between the traditional Yoruba religion of West Africa and the Roman Catholic form of Christianity.

The following are some of it's beliefs & practices:

- Each individual is believed <u>to have a specific oricha who has been</u> connected to them since before birth and who informs their personality.
- Santería's members usually meet in the homes of santeros or Babalawos to venerate specific oricha at altars set up for that purpose.
- Santería uses the <u>Lucumí language</u>, which is derived from <u>Yoruba</u>, for ritual purposes
- Offerings to the orishas include fruit and the blood of <u>sacrificed animals</u>, usually birds. Offerings are also given to the spirits of the dead, especially those of ancestors, with some practitioners identifying as <u>spirit mediums</u>
- Practitioners often present their involvement with Santería as a lifelong commitment.

During the next few visits I was given a light green and yellow bracelet called an Ide with a matching collar (necklace) of the same colors, which are the colors of Orula or Orunmila. The following are the beliefs associated with this Principality:

- **Orula** or Orunmila is the orisha of divination
- Supreme oracle
- Chief adviser
- **Orula** represents intelligence and wisdom

Orishas / deities spirits worshipped <u>native to the religion of the Yoruba people</u>. These are nothing more than ruiling spirits, principalities, demons in Satan's kingdom of darkness that he uses to deceive millions of people.

Here's important background when dealing with this principality:

- Orula is a strongman that must be bound first when doing deliverance and must be called out by its name, the pact that was made with Orula and the spirit of death must be renounced, repented and ask God to forgive you in Jesus Name.
- Every Ide bracelet that the Babalawo issues a rooster or whatever animal that is sacrifice. The blood of that animal is spilled on the bracelet and collares (Necklaces) while the Babalawo prays over them.
- The person wearing this bracelet has made a pact with the spirit of death.

Any ruling spirit such as:

- Orula & The spirit of death,
- Yemaya (**Yemaya** is ruiling marine spirit that has many names in many cultures who lives and rules over the seas and lakes. She also rules over maternity)
- Python, The Python spirit points to book of <u>Acts 16:16</u>, where Scripture refers to a slave girl who had "a spirit of divination." The Greek term for

"divination" in this verse is pythōna. The origin of the Greek word is rooted in Greek mythology

These are all principalities. So what is a principality in the kingdom of darkness?

1) a state ruled by a prince, usually a relatively small state or a state that falls within a larger state such as an empire.
2) The position or authority of a prince or chief ruler; sovereignty; supreme power.
3) The rule of a prince of a small or subordinate state.
4) Supramundane powers often in conflict with God. Ephes. 6:12.

This is exactly the kind of demon / spirit that Jesus spoke about in **Matthew 17:18–21**

Matthews 17:18–21

[18] And Jesus rebuked the demon, and it came out of him; and the child was cured from that very hour.

[19] Then the disciples came to Jesus privately and said, "Why could we not cast it out?"

²⁰ So Jesus said to them, "Because of your unbelief; for assuredly, I say to you, if you have faith as a mustard seed, you will say to this mountain, 'Move from here to there,' and it will move; and nothing will be impossible for you. **²¹ However, this kind does not go out except by prayer and fasting."**

Mark 9:25

²⁵ When Jesus saw that a crowd was running to the scene, he rebuked the impure spirit. "You deaf and mute spirit," he said,

"I command you, come out of him and never enter him again."

Getting back to my involvement in Santeria, after I was given the Ide and the collares (necklaces) of Orula about a couple of months later, the Padrino told me, "You need to get the guerreros (warriors) to protect you." The warriors, or idols, are the following:

- Eleggua Named Eshu Layore (which is placed behind your door; see Isaiah 57:8)
- Oggún
- Oshosi
- Ozun

I remember as a part of the initiation to receive these idols. I had to cut my hand and when that Babalawo created the eleggua idol, my blood was placed inside of it. About a few years later the first Babalawo I had his wife died from cancer. So about a month later I came by for a reading, and I saw a much younger woman on his bed in his bedroom. When he introduced to her, I realized she was a woman I had met in Puerto Rico. I had a girlfriend, and her oldschool Pentecostal mom used to babysit this woman's daughter. This women was a very nice young lady, but now she had transformed into a woman fully into the occult. They later married and ended up moving to Puerto Rico with his family, so I started to see his associate Babalawo who lived in New York. This Babalawo later revealed to me that he held the 4th highest ranking position in NYC at the time. The ranking was based on all of the various idols that he was initiated into among other considerations. I was not privy to know or was interested in. During one my readings the orisha (Principality) revealed to him that I needed another Eleggua, Because the original one I received with the guerreros (warriors) was constructed wrong. He then constructed a new one was made for me.

The next idol that the Babalawo was told that I had to do was La Mano De Orula, which is a three-day ceremony performed by three Babalawos, where they tell you your destiny. I was told during the course of the 3-day ceremony that Obatala was my santo (saint) and that I did not have to do the ceremony of receiving a saint; I could go directly to the high priest (Babalawo). The devil is a liar. I was not doing that meaning becoming a Babalawo. I thank God he kept me from making the mistake of being initiated as a High Priest and losing my soul forever.

Then after that I received the collares and osain charm. Who is Osain? **Osain** (also known as **Ozain** or Osanyin) is the orisha of wild plants, healing and magic in the Yoruban religion and its diaspora in the Americas. He is a powerful wizard, master of all spell craft and is found out in the wild, untamed areas of nature. In total I made the following pacts:

- The guerreros (warriors) Eleggua, Ogun, Ozun, Ochosi
- Mano de Orula (spirit of death) and the spirit of death
- Obatala idol
- Collares (seven African powers)
- Osain (good luck charm)

It is wise to adopt as a Standard Operations Procedures (SOP) any religion, organization, club, fraternity or anything as such that operates in occultish or secrecy a red flag should go up in your mind and make a mental note that it may require some further investigation. I say this because more than likely there is an occult connection to it.

Merriam-Webster Dictionary states the word Occult means:

- Not revealed : SECRET
- Not easily apprehended or understood : ABSTRUSE, MYSTERIOUS
- Hidden from view : CONCEALED

Jesus said in **Matthews 10:26 (NKJV)**

> Therefore do not fear them. For there is nothing covered that will not be revealed, and hidden that will not be known.

Note:

Palero is pretty much like a Babalawo in the Palo Mayombe religion, Which is a solitary religion, practiced secretly, with no houses of worship and no way of counting worshippers. Born of the ancient spirit worship of the Congo, it was brought first to Cuba through the slave trade, then later to the United States.

The following scriptures are direct reference warnings to the santeros, Babalawos, Paleros and those who create these worthless idols. But if you need further convincing in what is God's position on this topic then read Isaiah 57 in its entirety.

Habakkuk 2–19 (NIV)

Woe to him who says to wood, 'Awake!' To silent stone, 'Arise! It shall teach!' Behold, it is overlaid with gold and silver, Yet in it there is no breath at all.

Psalm 135:17 (NIV)

They have ears but cannot hear, nor is there breath in their mouths.

Jeremiah 2:28

But where are the gods you made for yourself? Let them rise up and save you if they can in your time of trouble; for your gods are as numerous as your cities, O Judah.

Note:

A lower case spelled **god** is a supreme being or deity, and it's spelled with a **lowercase** g when you're not referring to the **God.**

The year was 2010, and the month was August when my life began to change. I felt like what King Solomon described in the book of Ecclesiastes. King Solomon was the wisest man on the earth and the richest man on the earth as well. I could identify with how King Solomon felt, meaning he did it all, and it came to a point that everything he did became vanity; nothing pleased him anymore. I was for many, many years a professional DJ / producer of dance music and had done a remix. The music didn't move me like it used to, and the club scene was boring. I would drink myself sober, alcohol lost its appeal, and the cigars became disgusting. It was during this time I started to talk to God more and less to the worthless idols I was serving. I was asking God what was my purpose on earth. I was also asking God on a daily basis for many years for a family and wanted a daughter.

September 2010 A female friend of mine whom I had not seen or spoken to since April 1991, reached out to me via Facebook. After catching up almost 20 years of history she told me, "By the way the last time that I saw you about a few weeks later, I found out that was pregnant." I asked her "what are you saying? Are you implying that your daughter is my child?" I remember suggesting "We should do a DNA test this way we can be sure" So I believe it was now sometime in late October 2010 when we did a DNA test. A few weeks later I had just returned from a trip to Las Vegas for a

Marine Corps Reunion. I had a large envelope waiting for me in my apartment, as I opened the letter I had a sense that I was on The Maury Povich Show reading the results it stated 99.9999% she is your daughter.

it was all surreal revelation reading a document stating that I'm the father to a young adult daughter living in Hawaii. Simultainously I'm struggling with my own mortality with this strange feeling that my time on earth was coming to a close. I started to make request from God like "Please Father God give me more time". I recall saying "I know after asking you for a daughter all of these years, you finally give me one, I know you're not just going to take me."

I remember after a Saturday night in mid December 2010 of drinking. I woke up on a Sunday morning an started to watch Joel Olsteen. I don't recall exactly what he was talking about. But I do vividly recall at the end of his program, he asked the audience to repeat a prayer asking Jesus Christ to come into your heart. I repeated the prayer but didn't think much of it or if contained any power. A little while later I started to work on some music in my bedroom. I saw a transparent man walking quickly into my room; the thing is that I only saw him enter my room from his chest down. Then he disappeared right before my very eyes.

I believe when I confessed Jesus Christ as my savior my spiritual eyes were opened. But I had no one to explain this to me at the time. What are your spiritual eyes? It's basically being able to see things in the spirit realm like angels, demons, images, and whatever God wants to show you.

During this time I had a friend co-worker I had known for about seven years who would invite me to church, but I would never go, and she would continue to invite me, but I would decline. I believe God in his mercy and grace was trying to keep me from getting into dangerous waters. Therefore, I started to research on the Internet any information I could find on how to get out of Santeria, but I found none. The only thing I would find were things like its origins, history, and its various deities.

One evening my screen had this message: The animals that you sacrifice are sacrificed to demons! I was shocked, afraid, and surprised all at once at what I was seeing on my computer screen. The entire screen turn blue and the letters were in Gold. The crazy thing about it is that I tried to go back to the history to find this page, but I never could, and I never ever saw it again. It was at that moment that a small voice in my spirit said, "Investigate what you are doing."

I was led to research all religions, starting with Santeria. The internet at that time didn't have the information I was seeking. Even today there's no indepth deliverance book using the bible as a guide that could get you out the domain of darkness and also explain to you the truth at the same time. I then researched every religion not in depth but enough to sense in my spirit deep down inside if it was legitimate or not.

I searched and couldn't find the answer that I was seeking. At no point during this investigative period I spoke out loud what I was doing. I then started to make phone calls asking people hypothetical questions of how to get out of Santeria. Each person that I asked would say stuff like, "No, once you're in you are in and people would say "you can't get out." The devil is a liar, and I wasn't taking no for answer. I knew that with stuff like the occult you just can't play with these things. It's crazy, But I just knew you couldn't just throw the items out and go live your life. Despite me trying to find a way out, I would still go to the Babalawo's house for readings. But I would never ask him how to get out. Looking back it was as if I was gathering intelligence.

During my entire time in Santeria I was told that I didn't have to go through the normal process from getting the Mano De Orula (I'll explain later in greater detail) straight to Babalawo. Satan knew that I had an Apostolic mandate over my life as a descendant from the Tribe of Judah. This was why the enemy wanted to accelerate me to the office of babalaow. Something deep within me was very adamantly against me going any further in that religion. I believe in these last days the DNA of God's people is being awaken at specific times in their lives to fulfill his plan for a time such as this. As a matter fact my entire time in this cult I was always skeptical. I want to say it's because I was working as a correctional officer, and some of the training I received in the Marine Corps was to be observant, study your environment, and remain vigilant. Since a child I was drawn to things of God, to the Jewish people, calendar dates like "Yom Kippur," the Day of Atonement, and the Passover, and when I watched Biblical movies I would weep uncontrollably.

I remember taking my uncle (who accepted Christ before he passed away) to see my then Babalawo in some apartment in Harlem, New York. I recall he told me that his apartment wasn't available for whatever reason. The person's apartment was also a Babalaow a friend of the Babalawo assigned to me. He was about seventy years old or more. But what struck me as being odd and out of place was that the man's wife was beautiful and she had to be in her twenties. This woman had such sadness in her demeanor that it stuck out like a sore thumb. About a month later I heard that this woman had committed suicide.

I mentioned this because to me it was a red flag. Perhaps there are signs in your life that God is showing you that are telling you, "This is not of me, this is not what I want for you, come to me, I'll take care of you." There were many, many signs along the way that said to me to "come out from among them and I'll make you clean."

I recall during my last visits to the Babalawo, I was waiting to see him, and his wife was smoking a cigarette in the living room. I asked her, "Has anyone you know that was in this religion decided to leave?" She replied, "Yes, there's this guy that used to come here all the time. He stop coming, I see him once and a while he started to go to church." I was like, "And nothing happened to him?" She replied no. It's crazy that a couple of years later while studying the Bible I found this passage that describes her and him to the tee.

Proverbs 6:13–15, 19

> **13** He winks with his eyes, He shuffles his feet, He points with his fingers;

> **14** Perversity is in his heart, He devises evil continually, He sows discord.

> **15**Therefore his calamity shall come suddenly; Suddenly he shall be broken without remedy.

> **19** A false witness who speaks lies, And one who sows discord among brethren.

Once I was saved and started to study the Bible and I found the verses above and it took me staright back to the life I had in Santeria. The Bible was written over 2 thousand years ago and to see bible verse connected to actual people today was crazy. Specifically the following connection to people I dealt with in Santeria world:

- The Babalawo used to wink his eye a lot when he spoke to you.
- His wife walked by shuffling her feet smoking cigarettes and pointing her finger
- He stated on many occasions that he had to fight his enemies at 3 o'clock in the morning. I often asked what enemies, but he would never tell me. (This is the hour God often wakes you up to pray. Why? Because the witches and people in the occult use the opposite time frame when the messiah was crucified to attack the church with witchcraft.)
- These people lie to you. I have a Christian sister, and she was praying for me. The Babalawo would tell me, "She is cursing you; you're going to have to do something to her," meaning cast a spell.

The time had come for me to start calling people that I knew that are into Santeria. To asking them how do I get rid of the worthless idols, beads, books, so called saints, candles and get right with God. Every person I called said, "No, you're stuck with this forever." I would say to myself Negative. I kept looking on the Internet but found nothing.

January 2011 arrived. I was in my first year of a new decade, and a new child had entered my life. I needed a change. I was miserable and empty and didn't have anyone who could relate or help me. It was a fork in the road in this journey of life, my road to Damascus was before me, and I was determined to put this behind me and the life that I was living behind me. Damascus is a city in present-day Syria. It was founded in the third millennium B.C. Damascus was an important cultural and commercial center by virtue of its geographical position at the crossroads of the orient and the occident, between Africa and Asia.

The old city of Damascus is considered to be among the oldest continually inhabited cities in the world. So what is a "Road to Damascus" experience? It is when a person has a sudden insight that radically changes their spiritual beliefs. The original description comes from the book of Acts, specifically:

Acts 9:1–22 NKJV.
The Damascus Road: Saul Converted

> **9** Then Saul, still breathing threats and murder against the disciples of the Lord, went to the high priest [2] and asked letters from him to the

synagogues of Damascus, so that if he found any who were of the Way, whether men or women, he might bring them bound to Jerusalem.

³ As he journeyed he came near Damascus, and suddenly a light shone around him from heaven. ⁴ Then he fell to the ground, and heard a voice saying to him, "Saul, Saul, why are you persecuting Me?"

⁵ And he said, "Who are You, Lord?" adamantly

Then the Lord said, "I am Jesus, whom you are persecuting. It is hard for you to kick against the goads."

⁶ So he, trembling and astonished, said, "Lord, what do You want me to do?"

Then the Lord said to him, "Arise and go into the city, and you will be told what you must do."

⁷ And the men who journeyed with him stood speechless, hearing a voice but seeing no one. ⁸ Then Saul arose from the ground, and when his eyes were opened he saw no one. But they led him by the hand and brought *him* into Damascus. ⁹ And he was three days without sight, and neither ate nor drank.

Ananias Baptizes Saul

[10] Now there was a certain disciple at Damascus named Ananias; and to him the Lord said in a vision, "Ananias."

And he said, "Here I am, Lord."

[11] So the Lord *said* to him, "Arise and go to the street called Straight, and inquire at the house of Judas for *one* called Saul of Tarsus, for behold, he is praying. [12] And in a vision he has seen a man named Ananias coming in and putting *his* hand on him, so that he might receive his sight."

[13] Then Ananias answered, "Lord, I have heard from many about this man, how much harm he has done to Your saints in Jerusalem.

[14] And here he has authority from the chief priests to bind all who call on Your name."

[15] But the Lord said to him, "Go, for he is a chosen vessel of Mine to bear My name before Gentiles, kings, and the children of Israel. [16] For I will show him how many things he must suffer for My name's sake."

¹⁷ And Ananias went his way and entered the house; and laying his hands on him he said, "Brother Saul, the Lord Jesus, who appeared to you on the road as you came, has sent me that you may receive your sight and be filled with the Holy Spirit." ¹⁸ Immediately there fell from his eyes *something* like scales, and he received his sight at once; and he arose and was baptized.

¹⁹ So when he had received food, he was strengthened. Then Saul spent some days with the disciples at Damascus.

Saul Preaches Christ

²⁰ Immediately he preached the Christ in the synagogues, that He is the Son of God.

²¹ Then all who heard were amazed, and said, "Is this not he who destroyed those who called on this name in Jerusalem, and has come here for that purpose, so that he might bring them bound to the chief priests?"

²² But Saul increased all the more in strength, and confounded the Jews who dwelt in Damascus, proving that this Jesus is the Christ.

I applied for a position at my job that I had wanted for fourteen years and just was looking for a fresh start. Martin Luther King weekend, 2011, had arrived, and I went out clubbing for the last time. The music did absolutely nothing for me, and the alcohol I forced myself to drink was nasty and had lost its appeal. I drove my friends home that night. Just the other day my friend told me he remembers me telling him, "Danny, this is it for me. I can't do this anymore. I suggest you marry your son's mother and live your life because there's nothing here for you either." He said a year later his girl left him.

Chapter 2

THE ATTACKS

The attacks began a few days later. I had all of the classic symptoms of have a heart attack. I was on my way home from work when the attack came. I was driving on the FDR Drive during rush hour in New York City, in bumper-to-bumper traffic. I turned around to drive to the Brooklyn VA Center. The cars weren't moving, and I was panicking, living a terrifying experience. I thought, "This is it. I'm checking out; game over." I finally made it to the ER and was admitted. They ran tests and blood work and kept me overnight for observation.

The next day the test results returned: No heart attack! The doctor said it was stress and a panic attack. Today I can tell you with 100 percent assurance that it was a spiritual attack. The enemy doesn't come alone, especially if you don't know how to discern what's going on and who's attacking you.

That day the following demons attacked me:
- Spirit of fear
- Spirit of anxiety
- Spirit of panic

All ganged up on me to get me to stop pursuing getting delivered from that cult that I was in.

I remember it was a Thursday in January 2011. While at work I was in an overwhelming state of sadness, a spirit of heaviness was upon me, and it felt like a limp dead body was upon my shoulders. All of a sudden I felt this huge snake inside my body squeezing the air out of me. I tell you this had to be one of the most terrifying experiences in my life. The snake had my neck and was squeezing so hard that I could hardly breathe. I left work and immediately went to the Babalawo for a reading. I remember this man laughing at me like he knew what was up.

So he gave me the instructions to bring some fruit and flowers and go to the river and talk to Yemaya, who is a marine principality. So I went to City Island in the Bronx, in New York Orchard Beach area. I followed the instructions, asking for help, and left the offering in the waters. It appeared that it worked. I never felt that snake again. However, I know it was a deception. How did I know that it was a deception, I'm glad you asked that question. The only way a principality or demon will leave you is if you accept Jesus Christ as your savior and you under go a session of deliverance. Those demonic entities stay inside of you until you die if you're unsaved or until you get delivered (Saved). The that's the deception the spirit stays inside of you to keep you from your calling this way when you die you'll go to Hell.

The ruling spirit would command the lower-ranking spirits to cease manifesting themselves to give the appearance that all was back to normal. But I'm here to tell you don't play with your deliverance; make a decision to seek help, stick to it, and never look back. I will discuss later how to put all together properly.

That experience that I went through was the icing on the cake. I would walk in my apartment and look at the idols I had by my door with utter disgust and contempt. I was determined to get rid of these things at any cost. During this time I was unable to eat or do any bowel movements whatsoever.

By Super Sunday 2011 my constipation and being unable to drink much water was too much to bear. I went to the bathroom as I tried to relieve myself, and I nearly fainted. I called my friend from whom I had sub-leased the apartment that I was living in. I asked him to take me to the nearby VA Hospital. I was kept over night for observation and they conducted a battery of test to confim or rule out if I had a heart attack. Today I know if you go to the doctor or hospital and nothing is found there's a good chance what you have is something spiritual.

My last visit with the Babalawo I said to him that I didn't want anything to happen to any of my enemies. On my previous visits he instructed me to make a list of my enemies and bring him a hen, which was sacrificed. I remember his cold-hearted response. "The hell with those people; there's an old saying in Cuba, 'It's better for your mother to cry than for my mom to cry,' the hell with those people!" I just looked at him, and it was a series of confirmation after confirmation that this man and this religion were evil. Needless to say this was the last time that I ever saw him.

I was raised in Brooklyn, and if I had an issue with someone it was dealt with face-to-face, but to want harm to come on a person in this manner was not in me. If the person received some type of retribution for something they had done that's between them and God.

Just imagine you visiting people that you have known for fifteen years who seem normal, who are deeply rooted in a tradition that is in your culture, the neighborhood, and the music. I mean, you can go into any bodega (store in Spanish) and find some of the supplies to do your rituals; you'll even find these items in the big supermarkets. If you want to go even further, it has gotten to the point that even the restaurants, nail salons, and beauty parlors are no longer hiding their occult involvements with their altars out in full display. It all becomes normal—you become blind to the little things.

2 Corinthians 4:4 (NLT)

> [4] Satan, who is the god of this world, has blinded the minds of those who don't believe. They are unable to see the glorious light of the Good News. They don't understand this message about the glory of Christ, who is the exact likeness of God.

This is why you should stay away from the stores that have idols out in full display. The owners of these establishments have given offerings, sacrificed animals, placed spells over the very food that they sell. If you are still going to buy food in these places after all that is being revealed in this book. It is best that you pray over your food, break the curses, and cover your food with the blood of Jesus Christ. My people just look at the TV and movies; they're full of the occult, magic, and supernatural.

Remember that I stated earlier that I had accepted Jesus Christ as my Lord and Savior while watching Joel Olsteen. What I am about to explain is while I was doing my investigation & research on how to get out of that religion. I was required to pray to those worthless idols I had in my house. Every Monday night, I was required to blow cigar smoke, spray rum over them, bring them some type of offering and change their water. I also kept going to the Babalawo's house for readings, works, and animal sacrifices that he had to do.

This I was in violation of the Word of God after I was saved. But I did'nt know this at the time. This gave Satan the legal right to come at me. (This was the equivalent of backsliding.) This was the reason I was being attacked on the hand I accepted Jesus and on the other hand I was still drinking, having sex and doing what required with those idols. This went on from mid December until Superbowl weekend 2011.

I decided to take Thursday and Friday off work Superbowl weekend to figure out what I was going to do. I was miserable, full of remorse of ever getting into this cult. I knew there was a real God in Heaven, and I literally had a broken heart and a contrite spirit. I recall going for a drive just crying out to God, screaming, "I'm sorry, I don't know what I was doing, I didn't know the truth. I'm sorry, God, please forgive me, forgive me!" I was broken with no one to turn to.

Saturday morning I was determined to rid myself of these items and get right with God. I've already told you that I researched the Catholic Church, and deep down inside I knew they were a false religion. So I decided to call the Catholic church that my family and I went to since I was a child. I actually went to school in this church, and my sister did her communion there as well. I went there to do my face-to-face confessions with the priest.

So I call the father—I don't remember what's his name. He picks up the phone. I tell him, "Hi, my name is Dennis. My family and I have been coming to this church for three generations. I want to get right with God, I've been into Santeria and I've got these saints, collares. I need to see you today." The priest replies to me, "Listen, don't come here or bring those items here because I can't help you!" I was like, "What? Isn't this what you're supposed to do? To help people?" He was like, "No, no, no, I can't help you, I'm sorry." Click. I wasn't even mad because I knew that these people were not the truth.

Chapter 3

THE EVANGELIST

My mind at this point was racing a mile a minute. I looked up the nearest Catholic church near Co-Op City, where I was staying at the time. I found one. I believe it was Gun Hill Road and White plains Road. I called and spoke to a father whose name I don't remember and told him the same story. Now his reply was different. He was like, "Listen, calm down, nothing going to happen to you. Just get rid of the stuff and then come here." I was like, "You just want me to throw it out?" He said yes. However, there still was a small voice telling me not to do it.

All of a sudden I remembered my friend who was inviting me to church. I called her and told her, "Hey, Maria, I need to speak to your pastor. I need to do it today. I need to get right with God." She replied, "Let me call him and I'll call you right back." A few minutes later Maria calls me back and tells me that he's not her pastor, he's an Evangelist that when he comes to New York she drives him around because he has one leg. Then she added, "But he said that he's going to preach somewhere today, he's busy". I was like, "Please give me his number; let me talk to him."

I called him and explained to him my situation. He said, "I would love to help you, but I have to take the train to Long Island to go preach. I'm sorry. Maybe sometime this week we can get together." I hung up the phone and then immediately went to Staples to purchase some boxes. I went back to my apartment and just stated to grab every item that had to do with the occult and placed them in the boxes, books, ritual supplies, candles, idols, everything. I picked up the phone and called the Evangelist again and made him a proposition. I asked him to allow me to pick him and come over my house and do what had to be done, and I promised to drive him to Long Island to his event, stay with him, and then drive him home. He agreed, so I got in my vehicle and went to pick him up.

The Evangelist introduced himself as Jose Canela aka "el muerto vivo," which means "the dead who is alive." I introduced myself to him and gave him my story so to speak. He said this is what he does, destroy satanic altars. So the man begins to tell me his testimony. He starts by telling me that he used to be a drug dealer in one of the worst neighborhoods in the Dominican Republic. One day his rivals attacked him with machetes and left him for dead in the street. They gave him fourteen machete chops; one severed his leg, another across his face, defensive wounds from blocking the machete on his hands and chops on his body.

Jose stated that he was unconscious and he saw himself in a dark tunnel with these deafening sounds of people screaming as he was being dragged by unseen forces. He remembers when he saw at the end of the tunnel flames, he started to scream, "No, no, no!" Then all of a sudden a tremendously loud voice spoke that shook the tunnel and everything went silent. The voice said in a loud commanding manner, "This is your last chance! I'm giving you your last chance! You're going to preach my word!" I was just listening in a state of shock of this man's testimony.

When we arrived at my house my friend Maria was there with another lady waiting for us. Jose instructs them to come with us to assist him in what he had to do. I had absolutely no clue what was going on. All I knew was that I had to get right with God. We enter my apartment and I show him all the articles in the boxes and he asked whether that was everything. I said, "Yes, except for the things that I have on, which were the collares and bracelet." So he cut them off and started to pray; actually everyone started to pray. I started to cry feeling the presence of the Holy Spirit and he asked me to confess Jesus Christ as my Lord and Savior.

Immediately after praying the lady that came with Maria tells me, "You can not go back to the way you were living, because if you do, seven demons come inside of you, and you'll never be the same again. I tell you this because that's what happened to my husband." What the lady was referring to is written in Matthew 12:43–45.

Matthew 12:43–45 (NKJV)

An Unclean Spirit Returns

> [43] "When an unclean spirit goes out of a man, he goes through dry places, seeking rest, and finds none. [44] Then he says, 'I will return to my house from which I came.' And when he comes, he finds it empty, swept, and put in order. [45] Then he goes and takes with him seven other spirits more wicked than himself, and they enter and dwell there; and the last state of that man is worse than the first. So shall it also be with this wicked generation."

So let me explain to you what happens when a person accepts Jesus Christ as their Lord and Savior: the demons must leave the body of that person.

The Bible states in Ephesians 1:13–14 the following. Ephesians 1:13–14

> [13] In Him, you also, after listening to the message of truth, the gospel of your salvation— having also believed, you were sealed in Him with the Holy Spirit of promise,[14] who is given as a pledge of our inheritance, with a view to the redemption of God's own possession,

So now your body is the Temple of the Holy Spirit. You must pick up your cross, deny the desires of your flesh, and follow Jesus Christ daily. God lives in people, not in buildings. Those demons that left you are looking to see if you're really serving God. The devil will have his demons watch you to accuse you before the throne of God in the courts of Heaven. When a person sins and doesn't repent, these are legal grounds for those demons to come back in you.

So we left my apartment and placed the boxes in the vehicle and were looking for a place to get rid of these cursed objects. We drove around and around and finally threw the boxes away in a dumpster in Manhattan. Cursed objects are to be destroyed by fire according to the Bible. I drove Jose back to his house and made arrangements to pick him up later on in the day. Now I had promised a Catholic priest that I would stop by the church. I arrived at the church and went inside to have a meeting with this father. I just had to be sure what I was doing was right. My family were Catholics, and I had to be sure. It's crazy. There are millions of people on earth like me. I believed in a religion, customs, or traditions that were passed down from generation to generation just because our loved ones showed us. We never ever question the validity or the authenticity of these religions or even research what we're doing.

The priest asked me what did I do with the idols, and I told them I threw them in a dumpster. I asked him what are the steps to salvation. He replied the following:

- being baptized
- being a loyal member of the Church
- keeping the Ten Commandments
- receiving the sacraments, especially the Holy Communion
- doing the confirmation
- dying in a state of grace

I asked him to show me these things in the Bible. He replied we're not like Christians that everything that we do is written in the Bible. He also said, for example, when he dies he's going to purgatory to be cleansed for his sins. In Roman Catholic doctrine, purgatory is a place or state of suffering inhabited by the souls of sinners who are expiating their sins before going to heaven.

The priests started to speak about purgatory. Once in a while the Virgin Mary comes with her flowing white dress taking fresh souls with her to heaven. I replied, "Please, show it to me in the Bible. Jesus Christ paid the price on the cross for all of our sins." Then the father played a video of Clay Aiken–Mary did you know

At the point I've heard and saw everything I needed to know about the Catholic Church. I said thanks and went home to get ready to take Jose to Long Island.

I picked up Jose and started to drive to Long Island, and we were doing small talk. What I'm about to tell you is crazy but true.

I served in the United States Marine Corps for eight years and two months. Every year we were required to go through the gas chamber. Marines are given real time in a gas chamber, to teach them how to use a gas mask under extreme conditions. In the classroom, Marines are educated on how to use a gas mask and how it can save their lives on the battlefield if used properly.

The gas used in the gas chamber is chlorobenzylidene malononitrile, or CS gas, a non-lethal substance that is used in all branches of the military and police departments as a riot control agent.

Each Marine spends approximately three to five minutes in the chamber, depending on how well they cooperate. The Marines enter the gas chamber with their masks donned and clear, but once the doors are sealed, the masks come off. For their first exercise, they have to break the seal of their mask, which will allow them to breathe in a little of the gas, but just as the tearing eyes and the coughing sets in, they are instructed to put their masks back on.

The next step is to break the seal again, but only this time, they will set the mask on top of their heads. At this point, some of the Marines may begin to feel a sense of panic. Their eyes are now full of tears and the coughing gets worse because the gas is in their lungs.

The gas also burns the skin a little too, similar to a sunburn. Some of the Marines may refuse to take off their masks because they see the other Marines reaction to the gas and they fear that they will not be able to put their mask back on again. However, they will not be able to leave the smoke-filled room until they complete the exercise.

Once their masks are donned and cleared for the second time, they must then remove their masks completely and hold them straight out in front of them, but by this time, most Marines have a little more faith in their masks. They know that the faster they take them off, the quicker they will be able to put the masks back on and be able to breathe again.

As I was driving, I began to feel a familiar burning sensation all over my body. I didn't know what was going on, but I sensed it was some type of spiritual attack. I tell Jose in Spanish, "Hey, I think we're being attacked." I didn't know how to explain what was going on. Jose asked, "Is this happening right now?" That showed me he couldn't feel what I felt. I later found out that what I was experiencing was "Satan's flaming darts"

Ephesians 6:16, <u>NIV</u>: "In addition to all this, take up the shield of faith, with which you can extinguish all the flaming arrows of the evil one."

Jose started to pray and those darts were immediately extinguished in Jesus Christ's name. After the service I drove Jose home without further incident.

About a week later the Lord planted me in my first church, Pentecostal Church on 184 St and Jerome Ave in the Bronx, New York. My first pastors and the pastoral family were people on fire for God. My time at this church was approximately one year and a few months. It was here that I learned the discipline of fasting and constantly seeking the face of the Lord. I needed the discipline and fire of the Pentecostal Church to keep me in line coming from the world and especially the witchcraft background that I came from. My daily battles were intense with the domain of darkness. I can honestly say the reason behind all the battles that I was in was because of what Hosea 4:6 says, which is a lack of knowledge.

Just imagine going to war with another country with no intelligence on the capabilities of your enemy, how do they operate, what type of weapons they have, what are their strengths and weakness, and so forth. Let's face it, most ministries don't have the knowledge, wisdom, understanding, the oil (anointing), faith, discernment, or courage to engage in deliverance. I believe every significant encounter that I had with the domain of darkness is a lesson that people could learn from and perhaps won't make the mistakes that I've done.

The early days of my coming to the feet of the Lord, I was in what they call "Your first love stage." I call it the honeymoon stage: you just love Jesus. You're so excited that want to tell everyone in your family and your friends that Jesus is coming next week! The Bible now when I read it came to life like high-definition TV. I remembered my Bible would always open to the Book of Jeremiah during that first year, specifically **Jeremiah 24:1–7 (NIV)**.

Jeremiah 24:1-7 (NIV)
Two Baskets of Figs

²⁴ After Jehoiachin son of Jehoiakim king of Judah and the officials, the skilled workers and the artisans of Judah were carried into exile from Jerusalem to Babylon by Nebuchadnezzar king of Babylon, the LORD showed me two baskets of figs placed in front of the temple of the LORD. ² One basket had very good figs, like those that ripen early; the other basket had very bad figs, so bad they could not be eaten.

³ Then the LORD asked me, "What do you see, Jeremiah?"

"Figs," I answered. "The good ones are very good, but the bad ones are so bad they cannot be eaten."

⁴ Then the word of the LORD came to me: ⁵ "This is what the LORD, the God of Israel, says: 'Like these good figs, I regard as good the exiles from Judah, whom I sent away from this place to the land of the Babylonians. ⁶ My eyes will watch over them for their good, and I will bring them back to this land. I will build them up and not tear them down; I will plant them and not uproot them. ⁷ I will give them a heart to know me, that I am the LORD. They will be my people,

and I will be their God, for they will return to me with all their heart.

At first I didn't understand when he gave me this word. It wasn't until after the Lord had moved me to a church closer to home. I was traveling from Coney Island, Brooklyn, to the Bronx four times a week.

But it wasn't until I was in my second church Congregation, El Olam, in Brooklyn, New York, under Apostles Elbi and Lourdes Castillo. They taught me the Torah, the word Torah in Hebrew, means instruction, doctrine, law, from yārāh, which means to show, direct, instruct. It was during this time that I learned to dive deeper into the Word and research it in Hebrew not Greek to compare the difference. I'm not being biased against the Greeks, it's just that when Jesus was on earth, his language and culture were Jewish/Hebrew; he followed the feast, customs, and traditions of the Jews for a reason. The Bible states in the future the Hebrew language will be spoken when the kingdom is set up, and Yahweh's name will reign supreme, as shown by the following verses:

- **Zephaniah 3:9**. "For then will I turn to the people a pure language, that they may all call upon the Name of Yahweh, to serve him with one consent, "
- **Isaiah 19:18** "In that day shall five cities in the land of Egypt speak the language of Canaan, and swear to Yahweh of hosts..."

Getting back to **Jeremiah 24:1–7**,

The word Chaldean in Hebrew is "Kasdim," which means "of the Chaldees." It is commonly translated as Ur of the Chaldeans and is generally understood to be the birthplace of Abraham, "the Father of the faith."

The name Chaldea means: As demons; or as robbers.

The Chaldeans were known for astrology and witchcraft, and Nebuchadnezzar II is known as the greatest king of the Chaldean dynasty of Babylonia.

Since I was a child I saw my last name in the Bible, "Perez" from the Tribe of Judah, and wondered if my ancestors are from Israel. The Hebrew name for Judah, Yehudah literally means "thanksgiving" or "praise," "to thank" or "to praise." Perez's birth is recorded at Gen. **29:35**; upon his birth, Leah exclaims, "This time I will praise the LORD / Yah," with the Hebrew word for "I will praise."

since I was a very young child I loved music and I played several instruments. When I was older I became a professional DJ, did some producing and a couple of remixes in the dance world. I now see that this was always in my DNA I was born to Praise God.

The name is transliterated to English as both "Perez" (NIV, ESV, NKJV) and "Pharez" (KJV). Perez, in Hebrew means "breach or burst forth" and is named after the narrative of his birth as recorded in **Genesis 38:27–30**.

> 27 And it came to pass in the time of her travail, that, behold, twins [were] in her womb.

> 28 And it came to pass, when she travailed, that [the one] put out [his] hand: and the midwife took and bound upon his hand a scarlet thread, saying, This came out first.

> 29 And it came to pass, as he drew back his hand, that, behold, his brother came out: and she said, How hast thou broken forth? [this] breach [be] upon thee: therefore his name was called Pharez.

> 30 And afterward came out his brother, that had the scarlet thread upon his hand: and his name was called Zarah.

The Book of Ruth lists Perez as being part of the ancestral genealogy of King David, and both the Gospel of Matthew and the Gospel of Luke include him when specifying the genealogy of Jesus. It's crazy that a year before I met my lovely wife while observing Hanukkah the Lord tells her, "Your husband is coming; he's a descendant from the Tribe of Judah." I found pretty fascinating how God has been peeling away the centuries of lies of our true identity.

The Torah/Bible states that there's a scroll or book in Heaven that God wrote about all of the days of your life. God wrote this book before he even made this world.

"You have seen my unformed substance, and in Your book (scroll) were all written the days that were ordained for me, when as yet there was not one of them. How precious are Your thoughts to me, O God! How vast is the sum of them!" **(Psalm 139:16–17)**

Chapter 4

ROYALTY IS YOUR TRUE IDENTITY

The reason I put a little of who I am is because I honestly believe that before any born-again believer in Jesus Christ could engage in any type of deliverance / spiritual warfare, they need to know the biblical truth about who they are, the roots of your identity. I'm not talking about the roots in the land. I'm talking about the roots in a man or woman.

So we go to the Bible / Torah for the answer to all the questions about your identity. Most people when asked about their identity will say:

- I'm from this country or
- I'm that nationality
- I'm Catholic, Baptist, Protestant, Non-Denominational, and so forth
- I'm a Christian

The word "Christian" is used three times in the New Testament:

1) **Acts 11:26 (NIV)**
   [26] and when he found him, he brought him to Antioch. So for a whole year Barnabas and Saul met with the church and taught great numbers of people. The disciples were called Christians first at Antioch.

2) **Acts 26:28** (NIV) Then Agrippa said to Paul, "Do you think that in such a short time you can persuade me to be a Christian?"

3) **1 Peter 4:16 (NIV)** [16] However, if you suffer as a Christian, do not be ashamed, but praise God that you bear that name.

The original usage in all three New Testament verses reflects a derisive element in the term "Christian" to refer to followers of Christ who did not acknowledge the emperor of Rome.

What is the meaning of the Word Christian? In the Greek Septuagint, Cristos was used to translate the Hebrew (Mašíaḥ, messiah), meaning "[one who is] anointed."

Webster's Dictionary definition of Christian. (Entry 1 of 2) 1 A : one who professes belief in the teachings of Jesus Christ. B (1) : disciple The problem by saying, claiming, professing that you're in association with the following denominations just to name a few, because they all claim to be Christian:

- Catholics
- Jehovah's Witness
- Seventh Day Adventist
- The Church of Jesus Christ of Latter-day Saints
- Baptist (Example: The Handbook of Denominations in the United States identifies and describes 31Baptist groups or conventions in the United States.
- Protestant
- Messianic

This is why the world is in state that it is. Satan has managed to get humanity and the Church to focus on the color of our skin, where we're from on earth, the clothes we're wearing or denomination, and so forth. People seem to forget that there's been a war going on in the spirit realm since the beginning. Make no mistake, Satan has infiltrated just about every area in the world we live in. The purpose is to do the following:

- Create division in the body of Christ
- Water down the power of the Holy Spirit with false doctrine
- Keeping people chained up in the dungeon of religion

- Keeping people away from their true purpose and calling on earth
- Keeping people out of heaven

Satan has even infiltrated the food that we eat by utilizing embryonic cells. There's a list of companies that utilize to enhance taste, all in an effort to defile the living temple of the Holy Spirit (Ruach Ha-Kodesh).

Merriam-Webster's definition of "denomination" below:

Denomination: a religious organization whose congregations are united in their adherence to its beliefs and practices.

The word "denomination" is nowhere to be found in the Torah / Bible. However, in Jesus' day we know there were multiple religious organizations. The Sadducees and the Pharisees were two different religious groups in the nation of Israel at the time.

Each group had a set of beliefs and practices, which made them distinct from the other. In reading the Gospels of Matthew, Mark, Luke, and John, it's evident Jesus regularly opposed these groups. Jesus would regularly expose the false religious structures and ideologies of man.

At different times Jesus communicates that in Him, there's to be no division, that He came to gather the children of God into one and that there's one baptism into Christ—no Jew or Gentile, but one branch in Him.

It is written in the book of **Revelations 22:18–19** (NIV): "Warn everyone who hears the words of the prophecy of this book: if anyone adds to them, God will add to him the plagues described in this book, [19] and if anyone takes away from the words of the book of this prophecy, God will take away his share in the tree of life and in the holy city, which are described in this book."

This warning is given specifically to those who distort the message of the Book of Revelation. Jesus Himself is the author of Revelation and the giver of the vision to the apostle John.

Revelations 1–1: "The revelation from Jesus Christ, which God gave him to show his servants what must soon take place. He made it known by sending his angel to his servant John, The plagues of Revelation will be visited upon anyone guilty of tampering in any way with the revelations in the book, and those who dare to do so will have no part in eternal life in heaven."

We are living in a time where the Word of God is being twisted and manipulated to fit people's agendas. People are calling themselves titles that are not even biblical.

Even the things you see in church or the Internet must be filtered through the Holy Spirit to see if they are authentic. When people come to your church, your home, place of work, or wherever you go, you must talk to the Holy Spirit. Asking him questions like, "Is this your son? Is this your daughter?" Because the enemy of your soul is out to destroy you, your family, and your ministry. This is why our discernment must be at our all-time high. Your relationship with the Holy Spirit is crucial; you must be in constant communication with him, constantly talking to Jesus for his direction, for his approval.

Proverbs 3:5-7 (NIV)

> [5] Trust in the LORD with all your heart and lean not on your own understanding;

> [6] in all your ways submit to him, and he will make your paths straight.

> [7] Do not be wise in your own eyes; fear the LORD and shun evil.

Getting back to who you are, in the book of **John 1:1–4** it states the following:

John 1:1–4 (NIV)

¹In the beginning was the Word, and the Word was with God, and the Word was God. ²He was with God in the beginning. ³Through him all things were made; without him nothing was made that has been made. ⁴In him was life, and that life was the light of all mankind.

So as you see, your true form is light, not a color!

John 1:10–14 (NKJV), states the following:

¹⁰He was in the world, and the world was made through Him, and the world did not know Him. ¹¹He came to His own, and His own did not receive Him. ¹²But as many as received Him, to them He gave the right to become children of God, to those who believe in His name: ¹³who were born, not of blood, nor of the will of the flesh, nor of the will of man, but of God.

God the Father is on his throne in heaven ruling over his kingdom, through Jesus Christ the scripture states:

John 1:12 (NKJV) He gave the right to become children of God

So our Father is in heaven on his throne ruling over his kingdom, and we are his children. Therefore, we are are also citizens of that kingdom.

Philippians 3:20 (NKJV)

For our citizenship is in heaven, from which also we eagerly wait for a Savior, the Lord Jesus Christ.

Ephesians 2:19 (NKJV)

So then you are no longer strangers and aliens, but you are fellow citizens with the saints, and are of God's household,

The Word Becomes Flesh
John 1:14 (NIV)

And the Word became flesh and dwelt among us, and we beheld His glory, the glory as of the only begotten of the Father, full of grace and truth.

We're talking about Jesus Christ here. In order for you to truly know who you are it's necessary to go to the beginning in the Torah/Bible, not where you were born, not what nationality you are, what the world states is the origins of man, but in following scripture:

Genesis 1:26–28 (NKJV)

26 Then God said, "Let Us make man in Our image, according to Our likeness; let them have dominion over the fish of the sea, over the birds of the air, and over the cattle, over all the earth and over every creeping thing that creeps on the earth.

"27 So God created man in His own image; in the image of God He created him ; male and female He created them.

28 Then God blessed them, and God said to them, "Be fruitful and multiply; fill the earth and subdue it; have dominion over the fish of the sea, over the birds of the air, and over every living thing that moves on the earth."

Let's break this scripture down because it contains the keys to unlock many of the questions and issues facing humanity today.

God is the Hebrew word "Elohiym," which literally means "strength" and "power" and is usually translated as "God."

"Let us make man in our image." "Let us." What this is saying is that God and Jesus is being referred here as "us." Hebrews 1 verse 3 states, "The Son is the radiance of God's glory and the exact representation of his being, sustaining all things by his powerful word." The Word is Jesus as well.

Image is the Hebrew word "tselem," which is literally a shadow which is the outline or representation of the original.
- according to our likeness;
- let them have dominion over the fish of the sea.

The common translation "have dominion over" is problematic, above all because "dominion" is so readily confused with "domination."

Dominion is the Hebrew word "shelet": to have power, rule
- over the birds of the air,
- and over the cattle,
- over all the earth, and
- over every creeping thing that creeps on the earth.

So now each of you knows that you're a son or daughter of not just any king but the King of the Universe. The body of Christ needs a Kingdom mindset in order to rightly discern and tap into all that God wants to reveal to us, especially in these last days as we enter the greatest harvest the world has ever seen. As we continue you must know you were made with the following attributes:

- image, which is representation of the original
- strength and power

It's pretty amazing that if you were asked to describe yourself, you'd probably state, I'm this height, this color, with these features, when God has chosen to describe himself not with a physical attribute, but with the word Love.

1 John 4:8 (NKJV)

> [8] "Whoever does not love does not know God, because God is love."

Therefore, it is safe to say that love is not a feeling but a spirit.

John 4:24 (NIV)

> "God is spirit, and his worshipers must worship in the Spirit and in truth."

The world defines love as a feeling; that's what we've been taught our entire lives. Merriam-Webster states that the definition love is:

1. strong affection for another arising out of kinship or personal ties. "Maternal *love* for a child."
2. attraction based on sexual desire: affection and tenderness felt by lovers. "After all these years, they are still very much in *love*."
3. affection based on admiration, benevolence, or common interests. "*Love* for his old schoolmates."

The Word of God defines love as what is written in:

1 Corinthians 13:1 (NKJV)
- Love is patient,
- love is kind.
- It does not envy,
- it does not boast,
- it is not proud.
- It is not rude,
- it is not self-seeking,
- it is not easily angered,
- it keeps no record of wrongs.
- Love does not delight in evil but rejoices with the truth.

Therefore, not only we are made in God's image and likeness, but also our characteristics must be a vessel of love.

We also have the ability to create things by speaking them into existence:
- **Genesis 1:3** (NIV): And God said

- **Proverbs 18:21 (NIV):** Death and life [are] in the power of the tongue: and they that love it shall eat the fruit thereof.
- **Isaiah 55:11**(NIV): So shall my word be that goeth forth out of my mouth: it shall not return unto me void, but it shall accomplish that which I please, and it shall prosper [in the thing] whereto I sent it.

God has given every son and daughter the following mandate:

- Be fruitful. The phrase "be fruitful" means be productive.
- Multiply. The word "multiply" means to increase in number, and "replenish" means to fill or refill.
- Subdue means to control.
- "Have dominion over" means to have authority over.
- Over all the earth (meaning each son and daughter must have dominion over whatever area or sphere of influence that you were placed, whether it's in business, education, government, media, arts and entertainment, and so forth, you are to walk in holiness, full of the Spirit of God and letting the image and likeness of Jesus Christ manifest. Why? To Bring Godly change to this world by reaching its seven spheres, or mountains, of societal influence.

So why this is not happening now in our families, churches, cities, or countries? This was and still is the plan of God, but the fall at the Garden of Eden changed what God established.

Let's go back to **Genesis 2:7**: "Then the LORD God formed a man from the dust of the ground and breathed into his nostrils the breath of life, and the man became a living being."

Adam's name in Hebrew is "Adamah," translatable as "ground" or "earth."

The Hebrew ruach means "wind," "breath," or "spirit."

Here's something interesting in **Genesis 2:15–18** (NKJV): The LORD God took the man and put him in the Garden of Eden to work it and take care of it. [16] And the LORD God commanded the man, "You are free to eat from any tree in the garden; [17] but you must not eat from the tree of the knowledge of good and evil, for when you eat from it you will certainly die."

The Lord didn't mean physically but spiritually! The Bible states that we are three parts:
- body
- soul (your soul is what makes you who you are)

- spirit (it is this part that is dead from the day you are born until the day you accept Jesus Christ as your savior)

Let's take a look at what is written in **1 Thessalonians 5:23 (NKJV)**

"May God himself, the God of peace, sanctify you through and through. May your whole spirit, soul and body be kept blameless at the coming of our LORD Jesus Christ."

2 Corinthians 3:6 (NIV)

"He has made us competent as ministers of a new covenant—not of the letter but of the Spirit; for the letter kills, but the Spirit gives life."

This means if you just study the word and memorize the entire Bible and you don't fast, pray, and worship, you'll be operating in your own understanding and experience, and there won't be revelation of the Spirit.

Does God have a Soul?

- **Leviticus 26:11**(NKJV)
- And I will set my tabernacle among you: and my soul shall not abhor you.
- **Matthew 12:18 (NIV)**

- Behold my servant, whom I have chosen; my beloved, in whom my soul is well pleased: I will put my spirit upon him, and he shall shew judgment to the Gentiles.

Note: Every person born after Adam and Eve is handicapped, incomplete, not functioning correctly, in other words spiritually dead.

I remember the first time the Lord showed me what people really look like without Christ (not born again). It was October 29, 2012, at about 1:00 a.m. during the height of the Hurricane Sandy. I was standing on line waiting to get my car in a hotel in midtown Manhattan. I had to go into work at the Federal Prison MCC New York. As I was waiting on line, three women (different nationalities) came in and jumped the line to the front; they were intoxicated. Then all of sudden I went into the spirit via an open vision and saw what they really looked like. The crazy thing about it is that they looked exactly the same. The only way I can describe it is they looked very dark and resembled the chvaracter in the film The Lord of the Rings: The Two Towers the character Smeagol would say through out the movie my\"precious\"my precious\."

I asked the Lord, "Did I once looked like that as well?" He replied yes.

Let's take a look at what the Word states in:

Genesis 3:13–15 (NIV)

Then the LORD God said to the woman, "What is this you have done?" The woman said, "The serpent deceived me, and I ate."

> [14] So the LORD God said to the serpent, "Because you have done this,

> "Cursed are you above all livestock and all wild animals!"

You will crawl on your belly and you will eat dust all the days of your life.

Everyone born after Adam and Eve were kicked out of the Garden of Eden were born spiritually dead. This is why Jesus Christ had to die on the cross, so he can recover what was lost in the Garden of Eden. Adam e Eve's spirit didn't just only die after their disobedience. Adam lost his authority on earth essentially giving it to Satan.

Here's a key for you

In **Genesis 2:7** The **Lord forms Adam, which means ground or earth** in Hebrew, and in **Genesis 3:14** The

Lord tells the serpent you will eat dust all the days of your life.

THIS MEANS IF YOU WALK IN THE FLESH, SATAN WILL BUFFET YOU

Jesus said in **John 3:5 (NKJV)**:

"Jesus answered, "Most assuredly, I say to you, unless one is born of water and the Spirit, he cannot enter the kingdom of God.""

How does one get born again so you can enter the Kingdom of God?

The answer to that is found in **Romans 10:9 (NKJV)**:

"If you declare with your mouth, 'Jesus is Lord,' and believe in your heart that God raised him from the dead, you will be saved. [10] For it is with your heart that you believe and are justified, and it is with your mouth that you profess your faith and are saved.

1 Corinthians 15:20–22 (NKJV):

"But now Christ is risen from the dead, and has become the firstfruits of those who have fallen asleep. [21] For since by man came death, by Man also came the resurrection of the dead. [22] For as in Adam all die, even so in Christ all shall be made alive."

So if you walk in the flesh, carnal-minded Satan will have you for dinner. In order for us to be victorious, you must be born again and walk in the spirit.

What does it mean when you hear walking in the spirit? Walking in the spirit is when a follower of Jesus Christ does the following:

- Sow / invest their time reading, studying, searching the Torah, Bible, the Word of God. Just like a farmer plants seeds in his field, he'll receive a harvest. The greater the planting, the greater the harvest. (Sowing is also very important when dealing with finances. If you don't sow how can you realistically expect a financial harvest?)
- Fasting is denying your flesh, it's humbling yourself before a Holy God
- Worshipping is and activity that is often overlooked. God, I love you, Jesus you're wonderful, you're beautiful, I praise you, and so forth.
- Praying (especially in tongues) in your secret place with the Lord. Praying is a two-way communication with God, he talks, you listen, and you talk, he listens.

Many followers of Christ don't grow because they don't get the Word into themselves. If you don't give God time, natural voices will overwhelm His Spirit in your life.

Romans 8:13 "For if you live according to the flesh you will die, but if by the Spirit you put to death the deeds of the body, you will live."

Galatians 5:25: "If we live in the Spirit, let us also walk in the Spirit."

My people, when you're in prayer, occupy your rightful place at the right hand of God, in Christ Jesus; you're in Jesus, Jesus is in you, and you're both in the Father with the Holy Spirit, which means you are Echad, you are one, utilizing your authority as king/queen. Release the resources of Heaven to make a change on the earth.

Ephesians 2:6 (NKJV): "And raised us up together, and made us sit together in the heavenly places in Christ Jesus."

Revelation 5:10: "And have made us kings and priests to our God; And we shall reign on the earth.'"

As you can see, we must live and walk in the spirit in order for us to occupy our position in Christ. Now before you can truly grasp what the word is saying, you must get a true understanding of what the Father has given to us in Jesus.

The redemption in Christ is listed in **Ephesians 1:3–14,** and each verse has a nugget of gold for you to drop in your spirit, so get it into your mind and believe!

- 3 Blessed us with every spiritual blessing in the heavenly places in Christ
- 4 He chose us in Him, that we should be holy and without blame before Him in love,
- 5 having predestined us to adoption as sons by Jesus Christ to Himself
- 6 He made us accepted in the Beloved.
- 7 In Him we have redemption through His blood,
- 8 He made to abound toward us in all wisdom and prudence,
- 9 having made known to us the mystery of His will
- 10 gather together in one all things in Christ, both which are in heaven and which are on earth in him
- 11 In Him also we have obtained an inheritance, being predestined according to the purpose of Him who works all things according to the counsel of His will,
- 12 that we who first trusted in Christ should be to the praise of His glory.
- 13 you were sealed with the Holy Spirit of promise,

- ^{14} who is the guarantee of our inheritance until the redemption of the purchased possession, to the praise of His glory.

If you read the life of Jesus Christ you'll find he walked in the following:

- In him was life **(John 1;4)**
- and that life was the light of all mankind. **(John 1;4)**
- The Glory of the one and only Son **(John 1:14)**
- Full of Grace and Truth. **(John 1:14)** The word "grace" literally means "favor" in Hebrew
- "Rabbi" (which means "teacher") **(John 1:37)**
- He Preached the Kingdom of Heaven
- The Spirit of the LORD will rest on him
- The Spirit of wisdom and of understanding
- The Spirit of counsel and of might
- The Spirit of the knowledge
- Fear of the LORD" **(Isaiah 11:2; see also Isaiah 42:1)**

Everywhere that Jesus went he healed the sick, did deliverance, signs, and wonders. Jesus promises us that we will do greater things that he did! Let's look at the following;

John 14:12 (NIV):

> "Very truly I tell you, whoever believes in me will
> do the works I have been doing, and they will
> do even greater things than these, because I am
> going to the Father."

As I go from scripture to scripture, the goal is to paint
a picture of who we are. This brings me to the Hebrew
word "echad," which is used most often as a unified one
and sometimes as numeric oneness. Jesus prayed a powerful prayer that shows what was in the mind of God.

John 17:20–23 (NIV):
Jesus Prays for All Believers

> [20] "My prayer is not for them alone. I pray also
> for those who will believe in me through their
> message, [21] that all of them may be one, Father,
> just as you are in me and I am in you. May they
> also be in us so that the world may believe that
> you have sent me. [22] I have given them the glory
> that you gave me, that they may be one as we are
> one— [23] I in them and you in me—so that they
> may be brought to complete unity."

2 Corinthians 5:20 (NIV):

"We are therefore Christ's ambassadors."

The word "ambassador" in Hebrew is the word "tsir," meaning "one who goes on an errand." Very similar to the meaning of the word "Apostle" ("shaliaḥ"), literally "one who is sent off."

I remember when I was in my late teens I worked in a Texico gas station on 1st Ave in Manhattan, a few blocks away from the United Nations. We used to get all of the ambassadors and diplomats from all over the world. Many times they taught me that their embassy even though it was located in New York City, once you stepped into that country's embassy it was as if you were in their country, subjected to their laws. The ambassadors and diplomats were required to follow the local laws of the host country in which their embassy was located. It's truly amazing all these years later how the Lord was teaching the principles of his kingdom.

Here's a little kingdom terminology for you to see what Jesus spoke of, which is the Kindom of God and the Kingdom Heaven.

- As an ambassador you are an official envoy, a high ranking diplomat who represents the kingdom of God.
- The ambassador controls specific territory called an embassy (Church), territory, and staff.
- Vehicles are generally afforded diplomatic immunity.

Most Christians don't have the revelation or have the understanding of the authority that we have as:
- a son or daughter of God
- a citizen of Heaven
- a royal priest
- a chosen generation
- a living temple of the Holy Spirit
- an ambassador of the Kingdom of Heaven.

As an Ambassador of the Kingdom of Heaven, our Church (Embassy), home, vehicles, children, spiritual children, and property have diplomatic immunity. Any violation or trespass by Satan and his demons must not be tolerated. You have authority to expel Satan and his demons from where God has legally placed you to do the work you have been assigned.

Chapter 5

HOLD ON TO THE TRUTH

So what this is saying is that when a son / daughter is born again and they're fasting, praying, reading/meditating the Word, and walking in the Spirit, then they are seated at the right hand of God in Christ Jesus, Jesus is in then and they are in him, and you are both in the Father with the Holy Spirit.

High far above all rule and authority, power, and dominion of Satan and his kingdom, your prayers, decrees, declarations, and spiritual warfare are having great effect.

Getting back to being born again, understand that at the moment a person accepts Jesus Christ as their Lord and Savior, lots of things happen in the spirit realm. It's a process often called "Taking up your cross." You have to cry out to your God for the strength to hold out—for the strength to say no and keep saying no in the time of temptation. You must humble yourself and have the same mind that Jesus had: "Not My will, but Yours, be done." Doing this daily leads to:

Your transformation by the renewing of your mind
- conformed to the image of Christ
- walk in the same manner as He walked
- gentle and humble in heart.

Luke 9:23: "Then He said to them all, 'If anyone desires to come after Me, let him deny himself, and take up his cross daily, and follow Me.'"

The following are essentially very important things that you need to know, hold on to, believe, profess, declare, proclaim, decree over yourself, and speak into existence over your family, friends, ministry, and city. You need to be:
- forgiven of all my sins and washed in the Blood (Ephesians 1:7)
- delivered from the power of darkness and translated into God's kingdom (Colossians 1:13)
- sealed with the Holy Spirit of promise (Ephesians 1:13)
- God's child for I am born again of the incorruptible seed of the Word of God (1 Peter 1:23)
- the temple of the Holy Spirit (1 Corinthians 6:19)

- a temple of God, His Spirit dwells in you (1 Corinthians 3:16, 6:19)
- reconciled to God and you are a minister of reconciliation (2 Corinthians 5:18–19)
- set free (John 8:31–33)
- free from condemnation (John 5:2)
- changed into His image (2 Corinthians 3:18)
- a partaker of His divine nature (2 Peter 1:4)
- righteous and holy (Ephesians 4:24)
- a fellow citizen with the saints of the household of God (Ephesians 2:19)
- a citizen of Heaven and seated in Heaven positioned, right now (Philippians 3:20, Ephesians 2:6)
- part of a chosen race, a royal priesthood, a holy nation (1 Peter 2:9–10)
- an ambassador for Christ (2 Corinthians 5:20)
- God's workmanship created in Christ Jesus for good works (Ephesians 2:10)
- the light of the world and the salt of the earth (Matthew 5:13–14)

The Torah, the Bible, the Word is not only a living word, it's a legal document from the King of the universe. Satan uses every violation that we do to accuse us. This way he can have the legal right to come against every plan and purpose that God has us.

There are people that say that the Sinner's Prayer is not biblical. While in prayer the Lord revealed to me that by doing what is written in **Romans 10:9–10** essentially the person is giving the legal right to God to allow the Holy Spirit to begin the process of reconciling them to God.

I honestly believe that every person claiming to be a son or daughter of the Lord Jesus Christ should memorize these very important scriptures, which are the following:

- **John 3: 5:** Jesus answered, "Very truly I tell you, no one can enter the kingdom of God unless they are born of water and the Spirit.

- **Romans 10:9–10**: If you declare with your mouth, "Jesus is Lord," and believe in your heart that God raised him from the dead, you will be saved. [10] For it is with your heart that you believe and are justified, and it is with your mouth that you profess your faith and are saved.

- **Luke 10:18–20**: He replied, "I saw Satan fall like lightning from heaven. [19] I have given you authority to trample on snakes and scorpions and to overcome all the power of the enemy; nothing will harm you. [20] However, do not rejoice that the spirits submit to you, but rejoice that your names are written in heaven."

- **Revelations 20:12–15**:
  12 And I saw the dead, great and small, standing before the throne, and books were opened.

Another book was opened, which is the book of life. The dead were judged according to what they had done as recorded books.

13 The sea gave up the dead that were in it, and death and Hades gave up the dead that were in them, and each person was judged according to what they had done.

14 Then death and Hades were thrown into the lake of fire. The lake of fire is the second death.

15 Anyone whose name was not found written in the book of life was thrown into the lake of fire

You see the battle that we all face in our minds; it is here where Satan attacks. The Bible reveals to us in the book of Ephesians the following:

Ephesians 6:12, NIV: "For our struggle is not against flesh and blood, but against the rulers, against the authorities, against the powers of this dark world and against the spiritual forces of evil in the heavenly realms."

The Apostle Paul affirms our battle is spiritual, not physical. The enemies that we face are not people or objects. The devil uses those things as part of his attack, but our true opponent is not other people but sin. When we sin we give legal rights for Satan to operate in our lives. I've already told you that in December 2010 God revealed to me what I was sacrificing was to demons, and I confessed Jesus Christ as my Lord and Savior. Look at what the Bible states in the following scripture:

Ezekiel 18:4 (KJV)

> [4] Behold, all souls are mine; as the soul of the father, so also the soul of the son is mine: the soul that sinneth, it shall die.

God states in the text above that all souls are his, and the soul that sins shall die. The text below state that his people (you reading this are his people) are destroyed for lack of knowledge. What knowledge? God further states, "Because you have rejected Knowledge he's not only rejecting you but also as a priest.

The Torah / Bible is the written Word of God.

The Torah is the first five books of the Bible, which is often mistranslated as "Law." It actually means instructions. A Hebraic definition of Torah is "a set of instructions, from a father to his children; violation of these instructions are disciplined in order to foster obedience and train his children."

"Listen, my son, to your father's instruction and
do not forsake your mother's teaching [Torah]."
(**Proverbs 1:8**)

"My son, do not forget my teaching [Torah], but
keep my commands in your heart"(**Proverbs 3:1**).

The purpose of parents using the Torah is to teach and
bring the children to maturity. If the Torah is violated
out of disrespect or defiant disobedience, the child is
punished. If the child desires to follow the instructions
out of a loving obedience but falls short of the expecta-
tions, the child is commended for the effort and coun-
seled on how to perform the instructions better the
next time.

Unlike the Torah, law is a set of rules from a government and binding on a community. Violation of the
rules requires punishment. With this type of law, there
is no room for teaching: either the law was broken with
the penalty of punishment or it was not broken. God,
as our heavenly Father, gives his children his Torah in
the same manner as parents give their Torah to their
children, not in the manner a government does to
its citizens.

"Blessed is the man you discipline, O LORD, the
man you teach from your Torah"(**Psalms 94:12**).

Now if you're not taught or you don't study the instructions of God so that you can live and prosper, what you'll find is a world in the conditions that you find it today. When you buy a vehicle it comes with a manual that shows you how to maintain it, how to troubleshoot it, and what to do if there is a problem. The Torah / Bible is the same and much more, it's a legal book filled with laws of a kingdom.

Hosea 4:6 (NKJV)

> [6] My people are destroyed for lack of knowledge. Because you have rejected knowledge, I also will reject you from being priest for Me;

Because you have forgotten the law of your God, I also will forget your children.

The following text states the penalty to any person male or female who is a tarot card reader, fortune teller, spiritualist, espiritista, santero, santera, babalaow, palero, satanist, medium, or sacrifices animals to idols; the sentence is death.

Leviticus 20:27

> "A man or a woman who is a medium or a necromancer shall surely be put to death. They

shall be stoned with stones; their blood shall be upon them."

Exodus 22:20 ESV

"Whoever sacrifices to any god, other than the LORD alone, shall be devoted to destruction.

1 Samuel 15:23 ESV

"For rebellion is as the sin of divination, and presumption is as iniquity and idolatry. Because you have rejected the word of the LORD, he has also rejected you from being king."

Here's another violation in the scripture below I did for turning back to the Padrino and those worthless idols that gave Satan the legal right to attack me the way that he did.

Leviticus 20:6 ESV

"If a person turns to mediums and necromancers, whoring after them, I will set my face against that person and will cut him off from among his people."

Before I can continue I need to explain the severity of the situation that I was in. Actually a lot of my fellow

Latinos throughout the United States, Caribbean, Central and South America, and Mexico are in the same situation or worse than I was in. The following Bible verse really was the state I was in, and there are millions of people who genuinely love God, but due to their lack of knowledge they're trapped in religious systems set up by Satan to destroy them. Just look at

Titus 1:16: (NIV)

"They profess to know God [to recognize, perceive, and be acquainted with Him], but deny and disown and renounce Him by what they do; they are detestable and loathsome, unbelieving and disobedient and disloyal and rebellious, and [they are] unfit and worthless for good work (deed or enterprise) of any kind."

John 4:22 (NKJV)

"You worship what you do not know; we know what we worship, **for salvation is of the Jews.**"

Jesus was Jewish when he walked the earth; this alone is saying a lot. He wasn't Greek or any other nationality. Israel is God's chosen people. Many of you reading this book are descendants from the twelve Tribes of Israel. Many African Americans and Latinos are descendants from the twelve Tribes of Israel. Go in your prayer closet, and ask the Holy Spirit to reveal to you this truth. Satan has placed lies, after lies, after lies from generations to generations. It's time to rise up and allow God to use you to deliver your family like Moses delivered Israel out of Egypt. Decree the Red Sea opened and walk through the blood of Jesus Christ into the Promised Land. You reading this book, you're not witches, warlocks, santeros, babalaows, and such, but Apostles, prophets, evangelists, pastors, teachers of the Word of God, royal priests, kings and queens, who were created to rule the earth, take dominion in the area of your gift. Kings and queens own property, they have gold and silver not for us but to advance the Kingdom of God now, today on earth.

The awakening of the DNA of the descendants of the twelve Tribes has begun to gather the final harvest of souls. The reason why I started this book the way I did was for this reason. The mindset I had those six months before I was saved was totally different. I know of Jesus but that Jesus I knew before I was saved didn't exist. The intent is to take you on a familiar journey meaning wanting out of the cult / false religion world of witchcraft like I was in except with hope, answers, revelation, the truth, the protection of Jesus and all his angels, and a path to reconciliation with your heavenly Father. I suffered, fought hard, fasted, and prayed for ten years to bring what's in this book to you. If you follow the Lord Jesus Christ and trust him and leave Santeria behind forever, you will see God move mightily in your life. In Heaven you'll never find a santero, babalaow, palero, or an espiritista.

Chapter 6

STUDY TO SHOW YOURSELF APPROVED

Numbers 14:18 (NIV)

"The LORD is longsuffering and abundant in mercy, forgiving iniquity and transgression; but He by no means clears *the guilty*, visiting the iniquity of the fathers on the children to the third and fourth *generation*."

Exodus 20:5 (NIV)

"You shall not bow down to them or worship them; for I, the LORD your God, am a jealous God, visiting the iniquity of the fathers on their children to the third and fourth generations of those who hate Me."

Notice right away that God is referring to the sin of idolatry. God considered idolatry to be an extremely treacherous betrayal of a sacred trust. Idolaters were traitors to God's theocracy. Besides the abhorrent practices which accompanied idol worship in the Old Testament.

A new generation will tend to repeat the sins of their forebears. Therefore, God "punishing the children" is simply another way of saying that the children are repeating the fathers' sins. The tendency to repeat the mistakes of history is especially strong in an idolatrous culture.

I will use myself as an example. My grandmothers on both sides of my bloodline (this means on my mother's side of the bloodline and my father's side of the blood line) practiced some form of idolatry, witchcraft, false religion, and so forth. My mother and my father practiced some form of idolatry and witchcraft. I have already stated that I was a Catholic and into Santeria. How about my ancestors? It's safe to say it goes back quite a ways in my bloodlines. Who knows what sins and crimes against God my ancestors have done?

I know what I've done in my life, and I have repented for them. But there are things that you can not simply say, "Please forgive me for so and so sin I committed. It is only through the Holy Spirit that can reveal what exactly Satan is using as a "legal right" in the courts of heaven to accuse you and in some cases have legal juris-diction into certain areas of your life."

The word "sin" I have seen on the Internet as the acronym:
- S = Satan's
- I = Identification
- N= Number

The word "sin" in Hebrew is the word "hata," which lit-erally means "to go astray."

Merriam-Webster's Definition of **sin**
1a: an offense against religious or moral law
 b: an action that is or is felt to be highly reprehen-sible it's a sin to waste food
 c: an often serious shortcoming: FAULT
2a: transgression of the law of God
 b: a vitiated state of human nature in which the self is estranged from God

Definition of **iniquity** by Merriam-Webster
1: gross injustice wickedness.
2: a wicked act or thing: sin.

Iniquity in Hebrew is the word "avon." Its definition is: guilt, punishment for iniquity

Definition of **transgression**: an act, process, or instance of transgressing: such as: infringement or violation of a law, command, or duty.

Transgression in Hebrew is "averah" and is defined as a transgression or sin against man or God. The word comes from the Hebrew root ayin-bet-resh, meaning to pass or cross over with the implied meaning of transgressing from a moral boundary.

So I just gave you a little background of words that are very important in order for you to get a better understanding of their meaning. If you read the following scriptures you can see blood sacrifices are to demons. This is what happens when you participate in these acts:

- You're in violation of what God has established in his Word, the Torah / Bible
- You give your soul's legal rights over to Satan. How? By making a blood pact / covenant with Satan
- Your children are given over to Satan
- Your finances are given to Satan
- If you die in this state without repenting and accepting Jesus Christ as your Savior you'll go to hell
- An altar to Baal (to Satan) is erected in your bloodline where demons can travel from generation to generation

Deuteronomy 32:17

"They sacrificed to demons, not to God, to gods they had not known, to newly arrived gods, which your fathers did not fear."

2 Kings 17:17

"They sacrificed their sons and daughters in the fire and practiced divination and soothsaying. They devoted themselves to doing evil in the sight of the LORD, provoking Him to anger."

Ezekiel 16:21

"You slaughtered my children and sacrificed them to the idols."

1 Corinthians 10:20

"20 No, but the sacrifices of pagans are offered to demons, not to God, and I do not want you to be participants with demons.

21 You cannot drink the cup of the Lord and the cup of demons too; you cannot have a part in both the Lord's table and the table of demons."

This scripture above is a classic example of my people perishing for lack of knowledge.

I remember the Babalawos I knew would say on more than one occasion, "I'm a Catholic" but they participate in witchcraft. So they participate in two false religions: Catholicism and Santeria. I believe many of these people (meaning Babalawos, santeros, yagos, espiritistas) were called to offices of Apostles, Prophets, Evangelists, Pastors, and Teachers in the body of Jesus Christ, but they were deceived, taken into captivity as a prisoner of war (POW) and robbed of their true identity and destiny.

Note: Catholicism is often referred to as a religion of the eyes due to the idolatry. Meaning they need to see an image to worship / the costums they wear give the appearance of being Holy,

Now look at the people who won't enter the kingdom of God.

Galatians 5:19–21 (NIV):"[19]The acts of the flesh are obvious: sexual immorality, impurity and debauchery; [20] idolatry and witchcraft; hatred, discord, jealousy, fits of rage, selfish ambition, dissensions, factions[21] and envy; drunkenness, orgies, and the like. I warn you, as I did before, that those who live like this will not inherit the kingdom of God."

When a person gets initiated into the occult in this Santeria they enter in covenants, which are formally ratified and are usually sealed with blood. These covenants that people enter in the occult are illegal according to the Word of God.

Ezekiel 18:4 (NIV)

"Behold, all souls are Mine; The soul of the father As well as the soul of the son is Mine; The soul who sins shall die."

But the devil uses it to have legal rights over the person and his or her children. Satan goes to God and tells him that he has legal rights over the person and his or her children because they violated the Word of God. It's like you break the law by committing a crime and you can be placed in jail.

Revelations 12:10: (NIV)

"Then I heard a loud voice in heaven say: 'Now have come the salvation and the power and the kingdom of our God, and the authority of his Messiah. For the accuser of our brothers and sisters, who accuses them before our God day and night, has been hurled down.'"

Satan does everything he can to keep the person away from the Gospel of Jesus Christ, which is their only hope for salvation. I won't be surprised if Satan uses the place in the Torah / Bible where the violation is listed. If left unrepented and the person dies, Satan will erect an altar in the person's bloodline and go to the next generation.

Covenants are formally ratified and are usually sealed with blood.

A covenant is an agreement. Similar words are:
- accord
- bargain
- contract
- compact
- deal
- treaty

The word "ratify" (past tense: ratified; past participle: ratified) means to sign or give formal consent to (a treaty, contract, or agreement), making it officially valid. For example, "Both countries were due to ratify the treaty by the end of the year." Similar words are:
- accept
- agree
- approve

- confirm
- endorse
- sanction

It is time for you reading this book to stop Satan in his tracks. It takes at least one member to rise up and do what needs to be done to break down the agreement established with hell.

Acts 6:31(NIV)

"So they said, 'Believe on the Lord Jesus Christ, and you will be saved, you and your household.'"

Chapter 7

KEYS, TOOLS, AND PREPARATIONS

Fasting

Remember Jesus said that kind doesn't come out except by fasting & praying. Meaning that type of Demon doesn't come out except by fasting & praying because it's a Principality a high ranking Demon.

How long are you to fast?

The person being delivered and the person rebuking the principality out of the person should be on at least a twenty-one (21) -day fast. Do they have to be "NO" God does whatever he wants to do he's the one who will make that determination. The scriptural precedence can be found in the book of Daniel.

Daniel 10:2–3:

"²At that time I, Daniel, mourned for three weeks. ³ I ate no choice food; no meat or wine touched my lips; and I used no lotions at all until the three weeks were over."

Daniel 10:12–13:

"¹²Then he continued, 'Do not be afraid, Daniel. Since the first day that you set your mind to gain understanding and to humble yourself before your God, your words were heard, and I have come in response to them. ¹³ But the prince of the Persian kingdom resisted me twenty-one days. Then Michael, one of the chief princes, came to help me, because I was detained there with the Prince of Persia.'"

The Prince of the Persia and the Prince of Greece are both principalities.

It is so important to seek the Holy Spirit to assist you in identifying the name of the ruling spirit that you're dealing with. This is why I wrote so much about this one principality in my case: Orula / the spirit of death. The Lord revealed to me that Orula and the spirit of death were the main spirits I was dealing with. During my first deliverance session I was able to renounce, repent.

and ask for forgiveness for every involvement with every other demon, every act, every pact, every sin, every sacrifice, and every pledge.

During my deliverance session renouncing Orula / the spirit of death it's crazy I could'nt remember their names. My body was cold as a dead person and at then it was like I received a break through and shouted their names. I renounced, repented, and asked for forgiveness for my involvement with them, I renounced, repented, asked for forgiveness for every pact, every agreement, I renounced, repented, and asked for forgiveness for me and my family's lack of knowledge. Then I established a new pact with the Father, the Son, and the Holy Spirt from that day forth.

My deliverance happened after a year and a couple of months going to a Pentecostal Church serving God faithfully. During that year and a few months I had supernatural experiences, terrifying moments, battles with witches, manifestations of a dog covered in blood in this realm, visions with Yeshua, battle a territorial Giant, over a 24 hour battle with the spirit of unrest and so much more. Another book will probably continue what's written in this book.

I was Fasting, Praying and going to church Worshiping 5 out of the 7 days of the week and I had this Principality with legal rights in me. If this was me how many of

God's people going to church every week are in the same conditions or worst? The Church meaning you & I need to be so filled with the presence of God that we will be able to do what Jesus did here.

Mark 1:21-28 (NIV)

When the Sabbath came, Jesus entered the synagogue and taught. They were astounded at his teaching, for he taught them as one having authority, and not as the scribes. Just then there was in their synagogue a man with an unclean spirit, and he cried out, "What have you to do with us, Jesus of Nazareth? Have you come to destroy us? I know who you are, the Holy One of God." But Jesus rebuked him, saying, "Be silent, and come out of him!" And the unclean spirit, convulsing him and crying with a loud voice, came out of him. They were all amazed, and they kept on asking one another, "What is this? A new teaching—with authority! He commands even the unclean spirits, and they obey him." At once his fame began to spread throughout the surrounding region of Galilee.

The first step in your deliverance is to make a decision and stick to it; I believe by having this book in your hand you've made that decision.

Romans 10:9 (NIV)

9 That if thou shalt confess with thy mouth the Lord Jesus, and shalt believe in thine heart that God hath raised him from the dead, thou shalt be saved.

SINNER'S PRAYER (Say out loud)

HEAVENLY FATHER IN THE NAME OF JESUS CHRIST OF NAZARETH I come before you seeking your Kingdom & Righteousness. It is written in Matthew 6:33 "But seek first the kingdom of God and His righteousness, and all these things shall be added to you."

Father in the name of Jesus Christ I ask you to forgive me of every sin I have committed since the day I was born to this very second. I confess with my mouth & believe in my heart that Jesus Christ is the son of God and he died on the cross at Calvary.

I believe the blood he shed washed away the sins of the world.

I believe the blood he shed washed away my sins,

I believe that on the third day you raised him from the dead, ascended to heaven and is living and seated your right hand.

Jesus I ask you to come into my heart and be my only PERSONAL LORD & SAVIOR. Jesus please write my name in the Lambs Book of LIFE.

Father God I give you my life and ask you to take full control from this moment on. Please fill me with your precious Holy Spirit from the soles of my feet to the top of my head

"In the name of Jesus Christ."

- I Renounce, I Repent and ask you to forgive me Father God for my every involvement with Santeria & Espiritismo.
- I Renounce, I Repent and ask you to forgive me Father God & I Revoke Every USE OF MY OWN PERSONAL BLOOD & THE SACRIFICE OF EVERY SINGLE ANIMAL AND IT'S BLOOD TO CREATE ANY ELEGGUA, ANY MANO DE ORULA & IDE BRACELET, EVERY AMULET, EVERY CONPSUMPTION OF SACRFICIAL BLOOD OFF OF THE KOLA NUTS & CHICKEN HEAD IN LA MANO DE

ORULA INITIATION & RATIFICATION IN JESUS CHRIST NAME

- I Renounce, I Repent and ask you to forgive me Father God & I REVOKE EVERY AND USE OF MY PERSONAL BLOOD & THE SACRIFICE OF EVERY SINGLE ANIMAL AND IT'S BLOOD TO CONSECRATE & ISSUE OF EVERY COLLARE ISSUED TO ME, EVERY OSAIN GOOD LUCK CHARM, THE ISSUE OF THE GUERREROS TO ME IN JESUS CHRIST NAME

- I Renounce, I Repent and ask you to forgive me Father God & I Revoke Every BEVERAGE & FOOD THAT I HAVE EVER CONSUMPED AS PART OF EVERY INITIAN, EVERY RATIFICATION, SOCIAL GATHERING ASSOCIATED WITH EVERY PERSON PARTICIPATING IN THE SANTERIA, BRUJERIA, ESPIRITISMO & OCCULT FUNCTION IN JESUS CHRIST NAME.

- I Renounce, I Repent and ask you to forgive me Father God & I Revoke Every BATHING INVOLVMENT, EVERY SATANIC PRAYER, EVERY BATH WITH OMIERO, BATHING WITH BLOOD FROM EVERY ANIMAL SACRIFICED AND I BREAK EVERY PACT, EVERY VERBAL AGREEMENT, EVERY INVOLVMENT OF MY OWN PERSONAL BLOOD,

EVERY ANIMAL SACRFICED FOR IT'S BLOOD & LIFE FORCE. I DECLARE, PROCLAIM & DECREE IN THE NAME OF JESUS CHRIST OF NAZARETH EVERY BLOOD PACT WHETHER IT'S MY OWN, EVERY ANIMAL'S BLOOD, EVERY WORD I HAVE EVER SPOKEN IN SATANIC PRAYER, EVERY SPOKEN AGREEMENT, EVERY PARTICIPATION, EVERY IDOL WORSHIP AND OCCULT PARTICIPATION IS RENOUNCED, REVOKED IN JESUS CHRIST NAME.

- I Renounce the world,
- I Renounce the Flesh
- I renounce you Satan & everything you have to offer me.
- I Renounce worshiping & praying to worthless idols
- I renounce using the money you gave me God to use it in the occult. Heal & Restore my finances & Revoke Satan's legal rights to my finances.

Jesus, Please present my case before you as it is written in **1 John 2:1–2 (NIV)**; it says:

"We have an advocate with the Father—Jesus Christ, the Righteous One."

I ask you as my lawyer to present my case before the King of the universe and I make a new pact with you. I repent, I renounce and ask you to forgive my every sin, iniquity, and transgression from both sides of my blood-line going back to Adam and Eve.

Redeem BOTH sides of my Blood Line

Cleanse BOTH sides of my Blood Line, DNA, and genetic code with the blood of Jesus Christ.

Remove every unrepented sin, every iniquity, every transgression, every altar to Satan erected due to lack of knowledge.

Please Heal every soul wound that I have sustained and release the Dunamis power of the Holy Spirit into every area of my soul. Please make my inner man like Jesus Christ of Nazareth. So when the prince of this world (Another name for Satan) and his demons find nothing in common with them.

Revoke Satan's legal rights over me and my family. Everything that has been added, edited, perverted, and twisted by Satan to the book in Heaven that you wrote about me. Please reset it to what was originally written before the foundations of the world. I also ask for a divine restraining order over my life, my health, my marriage, my children, my family, my spiritual children, my ministry, my testimony, my property, my finances, my job, my business, and my home until the day of judgment; restore what was stolen from me and my family seven-fold in your name, Jesus.

Chapter 8

PRAYERS AND DECREES

Congratulations! You have confessed Jesus Christ as your Lord and Savior; great job! The next step is to properly get rid of every single item you used in the occult, in Santeria.

The Proper Way to Get Rid of Idols and Cursed Objects

The proper way to get rid of idols and cursed objects is finding a location away from your home where you can incinerate all the items, in a steel drum if possible. If not, do it in manner that no one else will pick the items to be used later on as a good luck charm. **Then burn all items completely**, clothes used in the occult, idols, books, bracelets, necklaces, good luck charms, photos, artwork, posters, Agua Florida, perfumes, statues (even statues of so called Jesus, baby, crosses, Virgin Mary,

Virgin Guadalupe). I'm talking about every item you used when you were in that world. The other items in your house the Holy Spirit will nudge you to get rid of.

Father God in the name of Jesus Christ you see the items that I have. I repented, renounced, and asked for forgiveness for all of these cursed objects I present here today for destruction as it is written in Deuteronomy.

Deuteronomy 7:25–26 (NKJV)

"25 You shall burn the carved images of their gods with fire; you shall not covet the silver or gold that is on them, nor take it for yourselves, lest you be snared by it; for it is an abomination to the LORD your God. 26 Nor shall you bring an abomination into your house, lest you be doomed to destruction like it. You shall utterly detest it and utterly abhor it, for it is an accursed thing."

I revoke every legal right Satan and his demons have against me, my children, my family, my spiritual children, generations, finances, and health in Jesus Christ's name. I thank you, Father God, for your mercy and grace in Jesus Christ's name. Amen.

Hopefully you were able to fast and pray at least twenty-one days before your deliverance session. In the mean time you need to get some supplies. What I'm about to share with and instruct you to do will raise the eyebrows so to speak from the so called deliverance gurus, experts, and theologians. The King of the universe instructed me to place this info in this book. The elements you see listed here were used in my deliverance by a man of God with over thirty-eight years in ministry, Apostle Dr. Elbi Castillo, Congregation EL Olam and Universidad Teologica Shema, Israel, and his team, which includes my current wife. We have consecrated God's altar, homes, businesses and have used the methods contained in this book on countless deliverance sessions; to God be the glory, for each time God glorified himself. I remember I was at my church with one of the prophets and a pastor praying and interceding all night until the morning.

The Lord stated that I needed to go through another session making it my second session of deliverance. It was about eight o'clock in the morning, and the prophet poured out three large cups of Manischewitz Gape Concord Kosher Wine. The prophet looked at me and told me, "The Lord wants you to drink these cups of wine because when you were in that world (the occult) you drank and ate things that were contaminated." I was like, "Are you crazy? Are you sure? If I drink this I'm gonna get drunk, it's eight o'clock in the morning and you know I don't drink." She said drink with that authority of God. I drank the three cups of wine, and I tell you it was as if I was drinking grape juice.

Go purchase the following supplies:
- a couple of boxes kosher salt
- one bottle of Manischewitz Gape Concord Kosher Wine or Welches Grape Concord 100% grape juice or Kedem 100% Grape Juice
- 100% Kosher Olive Oil
- Manischewitz Matzos Crackers

What you're doing here is a prophetic act utilizing the Word of God (the Word is Jesus). Remember you have made a pact with Satan and the spirit of death. In **John 10:10 (NKJV)** it is written:

John 10:10 (NKJV)

"[10] The thief does not come except to steal, and to kill, and to destroy. I have come that they may have life, and that they may have *it* more abundantly."

Proverbs 18:21 (NKJV)

"[21] Death and life are in the power of the tongue, And those who love it will eat its fruit."

Isaiah 55:11 (NKJV)

"So shall my word be that goes out from my mouth; it shall not return to me empty, but it shall accomplish that which I purpose, and shall succeed in the thing for which I sent it."

Job 22:28 (NKJV)

"28 You will also declare a thing, And it will be established for you; So light will shine on your ways."

THE SALT

Read this out loud when using in delivering someone and healing a home.

I declare, proclaim, and decree in the name of Jesus Christ of Nazareth on these premises, on this house, over the every area that every satanic ritual was conducted using blood and bring offerings to Satan and his demons. What it is written in 2 Kings.

2 Kings 2:19–22

"19 Then the men of the city said to Elisha, 'Please notice, the situation of this city is pleasant, as my lord sees; but the water is bad, and the ground barren.'

"²⁰ And he said, 'Bring me a new bowl, and put salt in it.' So they brought it to him. ²¹ Then he went out to the source of the water, and cast in the salt there, and said, 'Thus says the LORD: "I have healed this water; from it there shall be no more death or barrenness."' ²² So the water remains healed to this day, according to the word of Elisha which he spoke."

Father God in the name of Jesus Christ I declare, proclaim, and decree ever legal right Satan has in this house, on this property is revoked in the name of Jesus Christ, every portal to hell is closed, and every breach in my hedge of protection for my home, property, ministry, health, marriage, children, territory, testimony, finances, jobs, business, blessings, and provisions are restored seven-fold in Jesus Christ's name. Amen.

THE WINE

Read this out loud when using in delivering someone and healing a home.

As you are sprinkling the wine or juice over the same area where you sprinkled the salt on the place where the rituals were conducted or on a person going through deliverance, take a little wine/juice and put a few drops on the right ear lobe, right thumb, and right toe. Sprinkle some on the top and the side of your door and the threshold of your front door.

(**Exodus 29:19**). The laying on of hands was a symbolic act of identification. Then Moses was told to "kill the ram, and take some of its blood and put it on the tip of the **right ear** of Aaron and on the tip of the right ear of his sons, on the **thumb of their right hand** and on the **big toe of their right foot**, and sprinkle the blood all around on the altar"

This a prophetic act of restoring the person's ministry.

READ THIS OUTLOUD

Matthew 26:28 (NKJV):

"For this is My blood of the new covenant, which is shed for many for the remission of sins."

I declare, proclaim, and decree in the name of Jesus Christ of Nazareth what is written in Matthew 26:28 Over me, my wife, children, spiritual children, home, property, ministry, health, marriage, children, territory, testimony, finances, jobs, business, blessings, and provisions.

I decree over myself, my wife, children, family, and home as it is written in

1 Kings 5:4 and Joshua 21:44.

1 King 5:4 But now the LORD my God has given me rest on every side; there is neither adversary nor evil occurrence.

Joshua 21:44 And the LORD gave them rest on every side, just as he had solemnly promised their ancestors. None of their enemies could stand against them, for the LORD helped them conquer all their enemies.

THE OIL

Then you're going to seal it with the anointing oil. Take the olive oil and present it to God in Jesus Christ. Ask the Lord to bless it in Jesus' name.

Father God, in the name of Jesus Christ I declare, proclaim, and decree as it is written in **Isaiah 41:18 (NIV)**.

Isaiah 41:18

"I will make rivers flow on barren heights, and springs within the valleys. I will turn the desert into pools of water, and the parched ground into springs."

Over me, my wife, children, spiritual children, home, property, ministry, health, marriage, children, territory, testimony, finances, jobs, business, blessings, and provisions. In Jesus Christ's name.

Taking Communion

After being delivered and after you're sure you're living right you should take the communion at least every Friday evening. Just say out loud the scripture below and do what is says. You'll need wine, maza crackers, and anointing oil. Always confess your sins and forgive your enemies and those who have offended you before you take the communion.

1 Corinthians 11:23–26 (NIV)

"²³ For I received from the Lord what I also passed on to you: The Lord Jesus, on the night he was betrayed, took bread, ²⁴ and when he had given thanks, he broke it and said, 'This is my body, which is for you; do this in remembrance of me.' ²⁵ In the same way, after supper he took the cup, saying, 'This cup is the new covenant in my blood; do this, whenever you drink it, in remembrance of me.' ²⁶ For whenever you eat this bread and drink this cup, you proclaim the Lord's death until he comes."

Deliverance Questionnaire

Please answer the following questions to the best of your recollection and ability. Complete integrity is paramount no matter how embarrassing it may be, as it will assist to determine the best course of action. Start by going back to your earliest recollection in your upbringing up until the age of ten years old.

1. Were your parents married?
2. Was there any violence in your house?
3. Did your parents get divorced?
4. Was there alcoholism?
5. Was there drug abuse or smoking cigarettes in your house?
6. Were you ever molested or raped?
7. What religion were your parents?
8. Did your parents go to church?
9. Did your parents light candles or burn incense?
10. Were your parents involved in the occult?
11. Did you ever share your blood with someone as a "blood brother"?
12. Is anyone in your family with issues such as incurable diseases, fears, mental illness, or seizures?
13. Is anyone in your family a Roman Catholic, taking communion (which is *not* Christian communion), catholic confirmation, lighting candles for prayers, or attending a confession?
14. Were you verbally abused as a child?

15. Did your parents speak over you negative things, such as "You're fat, you're stupid, you'll never amount to anything, I don't know why we had you"?
16. Has anyone including teachers ever told you weren't going to amount to anything?
17. Did you participate in celebrating Halloween or any other satanic holiday?

Now from the age of ten years old to now list all the sins you have personally done; also make a separate list of all the people that hurt you and all the people that you have hurt. Utilize the same format as above, and if possible ask questions of your grandparents and ancestors, for example:

- history of mental breakdown
- chronic sickness or disease, barrenness, or tendency to miscarry
- divorce, family strife, or alienation
- financial poverty
- repeated accidents, any suicide or early deaths in your family

Once you have completed the questionnaire to the best of your ability and you're completely honest with your personal assessment for your deliverance, if possible find an apostolic five-fold ministry (meaning apostle, prophet, evangelist, pastor, and teacher). Pray and ask the Lord to send the person or team that will conduct your deliverance.

Father God, in the name of Jesus Christ of Nazareth I come before you seeking your kingdom and righteousness. I forgive all of my enemies and I bless them; I ask you to forgive and bless them as well in the name of Jesus Christ. Please forgive me for all of my sins and create in me a clean new heart and a renewed right spirit in Jesus' Name.

The person being delivered should do the following:
- Get something where you can put your feet in like a pan. So you won't make a mess.
- Put your feet in the pan
- Go through your questionnaire

Once you've completed the prayer, start from the top of your list and work your way down, for example:
- My parents were not married. I repent, renounce, I forgive them and I ask you, Lord, to forgive and bless them in the name of Jesus.
- My parents fought all the time. I repent, renounce, I forgive them, and I ask you, Lord, to forgive and bless them in the name of Jesus Christ.
- My mother was a prostitute. I repent, renounce, I forgive her, and I ask you, Lord, to forgive and bless her in the name of Jesus Christ.

- My father abandoned me. I repent, renounce, I forgive him, and I ask you, Lord, to forgive and bless him in the name of Jesus Christ.
- I was molested by my uncle. I repent, renounce, I forgive him, and I ask you, Lord, to forgive and bless him in the name of Jesus Christ.
- My teacher said I will never amount to anything I repent, renounce, I forgive her, and I ask you, Lord, to forgive and bless her in the name of Jesus Christ.
- I stole and did drugs. I repent, renounce, I forgive me, and I ask you, Lord, to forgive and bless me in the name of Jesus Christ.
- I masturbated, fornicated, and committed adultery. I repent, renounce, I forgive me, and I ask you, Lord, to forgive and bless me in the name of Jesus Christ.
- I had five abortions. I repent, renounce, I forgive myself and the person I created those children with. I ask you, Lord, to forgive and bless us in the name of Jesus Christ.
- I cut myself. I repent, renounce, I forgive myself, and I ask you, Lord, to forgive and bless me in the name of Jesus Christ.
- I did my communion and confirmation in the Catholic Church. I repent, renounce, I forgive myself, my parent or guardian that made me do this, and I ask you, Lord, to forgive and bless us in the name of Jesus Christ.

The person administering the deliverance should be lead by the Holy Spirit in using the salt, wine, and the oil.

- Follow the instructions of the salt, wine, and oil
- Once you finish the salt, wine, and oil,
- The person that is administering your deliverance at the end say in the name of Jesus Christ of Nazareth, "I bind the spirit of revenge, the spirit of vengeance, the spirit of retaliation, the spirit of death and every spirit that left the person (or so and so), you're prohibited from coming back upon me (or so and so), our family, every person and their family involved in this deliverance in Jesus' Name

While the person going through deliverance is saying these things out loud, there should be there someone praying in tongues, declaring and decreeing as led by the Holy Spirit over the person being delivered. It's good to have a prophet that sees in the spirit.

The person that was delivered must take the questionnaire outside and burn the papers

Let's do a recap

1) Make a decision, stick to it, start fasting, and get the supplies on the list.
2) Trust Jesus Christ will get you through it.
3) The deliverance team should be Apostolic and spirit filled.
4) The questionnaire is similar to when you go to doctor for the first time. The doctor uses it to formulate a diagnosis.
5) Remember you must complete the questionnaire with complete honesty and integrity, repent, renounce, and forgive. Then burn the questionnaire once you've read it out loud.
6) Declare, proclaim, and decree **2 Kings 2:19–22** over the one being delivered. Allow kosher salt to be thrown on your head, hands, and feet, while breaking all curses and legal rights. Renounce and repent every oaths, blood pacts, promises, animal sacrifice in the name of Jesus Christ. (Follow this same procedure on the area where a sacrifice was done in your house or business.)

Note: The wine / grape juice symbolizes the blood of Jesus Christ, and the olive oil is a symbolic for the Holy Spirit

7) Leviticus 8:24

"Then he [Moses] brought Aaron's sons forward and put some of the blood on the lobes of their right ears, on the thumbs of their right hands, and on the big toes of their right feet."

"These actions symbolize the consecration of you a Royal Priests' hearing from God, the work (of your hands) for God, and your walk with God." (Leviticus 14:14,17,18)

"He [the Priest] shall take some of the oil that is in the palm of his hand and some of the blood of the lamb and put them on the lobe of the right ear, on the thumb of the right hand, and on the big toe of the right foot of the one of you to be declared ritually clean. He shall put the rest of the oil that is in the palm of his hand on your head. In this way he shall perform the ritual of purification."

8) After you get delivered you need an on-fire apostolic church or blazing Pentecostal Church that's going to mentor you.

9) Get baptized properly and renounce any Catholic baptism, communion, and confirmation.

10) I suggest you don't waste time and get a good study Bible, a book called *Secrets of*

a Prayer Warrior, by Derek Prince to teach how to pray and for some e-courses and e-books (https://ryanlestrangeministries.shop/collections/e-courses).

11) Put on the full armor of God every day.

Father God, in the Name of Jesus Christ I put on the full armor of God.

- I stand my ground firm.
- I put on the helmet of salvation.
- I put on the belt of truth buckled around my waist.
- I put on the breastplate of righteousness.
- I put on the sandals of peace.
- I lift up my take shield of faith and decree all the flaming arrows of the evil one and his demons are extinguished in the name of Jesus Christ.
- I lift up the sword of the spirit, which is the Word of God.
- I bind up every attack, plan, works, and conspiracies in Jesus Christ's name.

I decree in the Name of Jesus Christ that no weapon formed against me or my family shall prosper today in Jesus Christ's name.